I0135136

 **inkslinger**

99-Day Guided Writing Experience

NightT
RiVeR
PRESS

Copyright © 2020 by Kimberly Cooper Griffin

All rights reserved. No part of this publication may be reproduced, distributed, or transmitted in any form or by any means, including photocopying, recording, or other electronic or mechanical methods, without the prior written permission of the publisher, except in the case of brief quotations embodied in critical reviews and certain other noncommercial uses permitted by copyright law. For permission requests, write to the publisher, addressed "Attention: Permissions Coordinator," at the address below.

NigHT RiVeR PRESS

Night River Press
880 South Saint Paul Street
Denver CO 80209
skeetieb@me.com
www.nightriverpress.com

Ordering Information:
Quantity sales. Special discounts are available on quantity purchases by corporations, associations, and others. For details, contact the publisher at the address above.

Printed in the United States of America
Paperback Cover: ISBN 978-0-9964349-5-9
Ebook: ISBN 978-0-9964349-4-2

Library of Congress Control Number: 2020946235

Contributor: Skeeter Buck
Editor: Marlo Garnsworthy
Cover Designer & Graphics: Shelle Pourmanafzadehardabili

inkslinger
99-Day Guided Writing Experience

A Guide to
Writing a Book in 99 Days

TABLE OF CONTENTS

Introduction 5

Part I - Before You Start Slinging the Ink 11

Inspiration 15
  Things Most Writers Want to Know 19
  Target Audience 27
  Genre 33
  Text Elements: Fiction 35
  Story Arc and Plot 37
  Point of View (POV) 41
  Outline - Fiction 47
  Setting 51
  Character Sketches 55
  Conflict 59
  Rising Action and Creating Tension 63
  The Climax 67
  The Falling Action 69
  Resolution, Also Fancily Known as the Denouement ... 71
  Text Elements: Nonfiction 73
  Types of Nonfiction 75
  Nonfiction Text Structures 79

Perspiration 85
  Writing Starts with an Ugly First Draft 89
  Progress 95
  Research 99
  The Hook 103
  Show, Don't Tell 107

Transformation 109
  Rewrites, Revisions, Self-edits, Oh My! 111
  Motivation 119

Part II - Inkslinger 99-Day Guided Path.......125

**Your Inkslinger – 99-Day Guided
Writing Experience**.................................**129**

Days One through Five – Inspiration..............131
Day One 134
Day Two 136
Day Three 135
Day Four..138
Day Five 140
Days Six through Eighty-five - Perspiration.........143
Words Needed Per Day to Reach 50,000 145
Sample Calendar 147
Day Eighty-six—Celebration.....................151
Days Eighty-seven through Ninety-nine—
Transformation 152

What Comes Next?.............................**155**

Deciding Not to Publish.........................157
Self-publishing.................................159
Traditional Publishing..........................161
Boutique Publishing or Hybrid Publishing 163

Before you go **165**

Inkslinger (noun) - a writer, a scribbler

Merriam-Webster.com Dictionary, Merriam-Webster, http://www.merriam-webster.com/inkslinger. Accessed 29 Jul. 2020

Introduction

Welcome to Inkslinger—
99-Day Guided Writing Experience!

We're so excited you've decided to write your story.

Did you know that, according to a recent survey, eighty-one percent of people who responded said they have a book inside them? That's *four out of every five people* walking around with a story to tell. Yet only a small fraction of people ever actually do write a book in their lifetime.

There are all kinds of reasons most people never end up creating the stories they dream of writing. Some don't have the time. Others say they have too many distractions. Still others aren't sure anyone would ever read what they want to write. But the number one reason people don't write their books is simple: **they don't think they know *how*.**

So, they don't.

And that's a dang shame.

Countless great stories have never been told because the people who wanted to tell them thought the writing process was beyond their capabilities.

The thing is, writing a book isn't a precise formula. No two authors have the same process. No two authors possess the same talent. Believe it or not, many authors didn't even go to school to learn how to become great writers. Some writers can't even tell you how they write their books; they just do it. They put pen to paper, fingers to keyboard, or voice to dictation program, and they write until the story that's been tumbling around inside their mind is written.

And maybe that last kind of writer is the luckiest kind of writer. They don't overthink it. They don't get overwhelmed by all the details, the "right" processes, the things they don't know. They just do it. That's what writing a book is—it's about simply getting the words written so someone else can enjoy the story.

We aren't going to lie to you, though. There are certain elements that make some books better than others. Those elements can be different from book to book. What worked for one story may not work for another. And, as we all know, not every book will appeal to every reader. But if you worry too much about all that stuff, about all the things you don't know, or how you compare to other authors, or whether or not people will like your story, you'll find it harder to get your story written...or maybe never even start.

We'll let you in on a secret about writing. The number one thing a writer must do is:

> # *Write the story*

We just blew your mind, right?

Wait. That can't be the secret, you say. There has to be more to it, you say.

Well, there isn't. The secret to being an author is truly to just write the story. Easy to say, we know. Sure, it takes work, and when you're finished, there are many things to be done to polish the story to make it publishable. But here's a great quote by a prolific novelist and short story writer, and—get this—she even writes issues of *Wonder Woman*.

> *"You might not write well every day, but you can always edit a bad page. You can't edit a blank page."*
> ~ **Jodi Picoult**

Think about that for a few seconds.

"You can't edit a blank page."

That's permission right there. Permission to give it a shot. Permission to *not* expect great words in your first draft. Permission to just get the story out and *then* worry about making it great.

There is certain knowledge you may or may not have that will make writing your story easier or harder to accomplish, but the thing is the magic of storytelling is not in the technical skills a writer has. It's actually in the writer's imagination and getting the story written. The technical skills will come in time if you keep at it.

We want to hear your stories! The *world* needs your stories!

We are committed to making the process accessible for any person who wants to write their story.

Our job in putting together the *Inkslinger – 99-Day Writing Experience* is to give you the framework in which to get your book written. To help accomplish this, we provide lots of educational information to assist you along on your journey. We also ease your worries about not knowing all the technical skills needed to produce solid work. In addition, we'll give you a 99-day schedule that will guide you through the process. Heck, we'll even throw in some ideas on how to keep you going when it feels like you may have bitten off more than you can chew.

Sound good? We hope so!

Your job on this journey is two-fold: bring your story idea and commit to a schedule that will help you successfully write a 50,000-word first draft of the book you've always wanted to write. That's it. Admittedly, it's actually a lot. But we know you can do it. Your desire to be a writer is going to help you do it, and we'll be here, cheering you on.

Finally, writing is art. It's a creative endeavor. Have fun with it. Let go of the things that try to limit you. Embrace your inner Inkslinger and tell the story that wants to be told!

What will you have at the end of 99 days?

A fifty-thousand-word revised draft of a manuscript that is ready to be sent to a professional editor.

Get ready to write your amazing book!

Part I - Before You Start Slinging the Ink

Part I is broken into four sections that prepare you for the *Inkslinger – 99-Day Guided Writing Experience.*

Inspiration – Planning your story

Perspiration – Writing your story

Transformation – Smoothing out your story

Motivation – Keep writing your story when things get hard

In the introduction, we told you the secret to writing a book is:

Write the story!

Sounds simple, right?

It really is, especially for those who have already written a book and know all the things that go into it, or those who have decided not to worry about all the things they don't know about writing. If that's the case, you can skip to Part II, which is where we get you set up on the *Inkslinger 99-Day Guided Path*. All the information and helpful tips will still be here in Part I if you want to check them out later. If you're ready to start writing, do it! Don't let anything get in the way of your creativity.

But if you want to do a little preparation, this is a great section for you.

In this section, we'll tell you a little about a lot of things. Don't worry. There won't be a test at the end, and you won't have to be an expert at any of the things we tell you about. What we go over in this section will be just enough to scratch the surface of the basics, so you know how to deal with them as you write your *Inkslinger* project. The cool thing is, after you read about these items, they'll still be here for you to come back to if you have a question while you're slinging the ink.

Before we get started, something we want to acknowledge is that the process of writing is a deeply personal act for writers. Whether you are here to create the next literary masterpiece or looking for guidance on how to tell a good story, there are a set of general steps that go into writing a book, and while they don't need to be followed precisely, it helps to at least understand the general idea of them. Writing is a creative process, and not all stories follow the same format. In fact, some stories are successful *because* they don't follow the expected format at all. But in order to go outside the norm, one must understand the norm so one can successfully bend the rules.

This section goes through many—but definitely not all—the key components of writing a novel. We go over things like plot, story arcs, and genre. We provide ideas on how to use them in your project. We've also created worksheets, which you will find in *Part II - Inkslinger 99-Day Guided Path* section, as well as in the appendix, to help you come up with ways to incorporate all of this into your story if it helps you.

We have defined a solid checklist of items that will propel an inspired writer to complete a 50,000-word manuscript in 99 days. There are more items that can be added to the list, but if a writer were to follow this guideline, and adhere to the 99-day schedule, they could successfully complete their manuscript in 99 days.

Are you ready?

Well, let's get started, shall we?

Inspiration

To write a book, one must be inspired. Inspired about a story. Inspired about an idea. Inspired about being inspired. It doesn't matter what your inspiration is, it's all about being inspired enough to write a book about it.

If you aren't inspired, it will be awfully hard to write 50,000 words. It can be done, but dang! That's a lot of words to slog through if you don't feel strongly about whatever it is you're writing. Also, if you don't feel strongly about it, chances are readers are going to pick up on that and not feel strongly enough about it to read it. And a book without readers might as well be a doorstop. So, in that respect, inspiration is a key factor in writing an interesting book.

What is inspiration then, and how do you get it if you haven't already gotten it?

We love this definition of inspiration from Merriam-Webster's Dictionary:

> **Inspiration** - *a divine influence or action on a person believed to qualify [them] to receive and communicate a sacred revelation.*

Marinate on that for a minute. That **sacred revelation** is the topic of your book, and you have been **divinely influenced.** You *have* to write it!

But how do you get inspiration? Well, simply put, inspiration comes in different forms for everyone.

It can come in the form of a great epiphany or in the witnessing of a simple, everyday action. It can come in a flash or over the course of days or weeks or years. It can be a surprise, or it can be completely scripted. The main thing about inspiration is you need to be *open* to being struck by it in order to get it.

Many people who want to write a book have already been inspired by an idea, and they want to write about it. And some people want to write a book, but they have not yet been inspired by a specific concept or story they want to write about. What do you do then?

You go out into the world and look for inspiration. That actually works for some people. It can be daunting, as well as take a lot of time, but it's an option.

Another way—and probably much quicker—is to go onto the Internet and Google "writing prompt generators." These are simple applications that have been written by developers to generate ideas for stories. There are a ton of them out there. Why is that? Because there are a lot of writers looking for inspiration. So, if that's you, know you're in good company! Go check some of them out and keep hitting the generate button until you find a topic that interests you.

Not into the writing prompt generator thing? Not to worry! Some of the best stories have come from ideas pulled from thin air. For instance, Mary Shelley described her inspiration for the masterpiece horror novel *Frankenstein* in the introduction to her novel: "When I placed my head on my pillow, I saw — with shut eyes, but acute mental vision — the pale student of unhallowed arts kneeling beside the thing he had put together." Can you imagine that? A vision of horror came to her mind and she just *needed* to write about it.

And Robert Louis Stevenson came up with the story of *The Strange Case of Dr. Jekyll and Mr. Hyde* from a nightmare. Whoa! What a nightmare! A nightmare that spawned a classic novel, several movies, and countless ideas for related stories.

The point is, inspiration can come from anywhere and you never know how widely your small idea can expand once you give it to the world.

Once you feel what inspiration feels like, it usually comes easier. Over time, you may not even need the help.

Things Most Writers Want to Know Before Writing a Book

This is where we answer some of your most nagging questions.

As we said near the beginning, there are some things a new writer wants to know before writing a book. These are the things that help orient them in the process. Most people don't feel comfortable jumping into a new pursuit without knowing a little something about it first, and writing is no different. We spent some time asking new writers some of the things that they want to know or wished they had known before getting started. Believe it or not, most of it was not about the technical skills needed to write a book. It was about wanting to understand the process.

Here are a few of the most common questions we received.

How long does it take to write a book?

Check out the list below to see how long it took some well-known authors to write their famous books. As you can see, the answer to this question varies widely from writer to writer and story to story. There are so many things that can contribute to the timeline of writing a story, that it's difficult to predict how long it will take any individual writer to write their story. That's one of the reasons we decided to create the ***Inkslinger – 99-Day Guided Writing Experience***. By taking away some of the unknowns and creating a schedule, we can provide a predictable process. In this way, *you* can write your story in 99 days.

Title	Author	Word Count	Time to Write
On the Road	Jack Kerouac	96,860	21 days
A Clockwork Orange	Anthony Burgess	67,280	21 days
A Christmas Carol	Charles Dickens	27,405	6 weeks
As I Lay Dying	William Faulkner	66,750	6 weeks
Casino Royal	Ian Fleming	43,790	2 months
Twilight	Stephanie Meyer	111,795	3 months
Wuthering Heights	Emily Bronte	118,465	9 months
Frankenstein	Mary Shelley	90,625	1 year
The Jungle Book	Rudyard Kipling	19,575	1.5 years
Fifty Shades Trilogy	E. L. James	519,100	1.5 years
David Copperfield	Charles Dickens	138,000	19 months
Golden Compass	Phillip Pullman	140,000	2 years
The Great Gatsby	F. Scott Fitzgerald	47,094	2.5 years
Gone Girl	Gillian Flynn	167,910	3 years
A Game of Thrones	George R. R. Martin	293,770	5 years
Lord of the Flies	William Golding	60,755	5 years
Gone with the Wind	Margaret Mitchell	426,590	10years
Les Miserables	Victor Hugo	545,925	12 years
Lord of the Rings Trilogy	J. R. R. Tolkien	432,000	16 years

What is the normal length for a book?

Certain genres have accepted word count ranges. The ranges have been established over time by writers and publishers, and readers of various genres have come to expect to buy books within the expected word counts. As you can see in the above list, there are certainly exceptions to rules, though. In today's publishing environment, where many writers have chosen to self-publish, many writers subscribe to "the story takes as many words to write as it needs to get the story told," attitude. Therefore, desired length usually comes into play based on what you plan to do with the story when you finish writing it.

Our advice for the first-time writer is to do the research on word count guidelines for your particular genre and if you know the publishing route you plan to take, adhere to any posted requirements. However, while writing, try not to worry about the length as you write the first draft. Just let the story take life. You can always edit it for length later. And always remember, rules are made to be broken. Just know that the more experience you have at this, the easier it is to get away with it.

Inkslinger – 99-Day Guided Writing Experience is set to 50,000 words, which is a good goal to start with.

Word Count Guide

Category	Average Word Count
Fiction	
Crime	70,000 to 90,000
Fantasy	90,000 to 120,000
Historical	80,000 to 120,000
Horror	80,000 to 120,000
Middle Grade	20,000 to 50,000
Mystery	70,000 to 90,000
New Adult	60,000 to 85,000
Paranormal	85,000 to 100,000
Romance	50,000 to 100,000
Sci-Fi	90,000 to 120,000
Thriller	70,000 to 90,000
Urban Fantasy	70,000 to 90,000
Young Adult	50,000 to 80,000
Nonfiction	
Biography	50,000 to 110,000
Devotional	30,000 to 50,000
How-To	40,000 to 50,000
Memoir	50,000 to 90,000
Narrative Nonfiction	50,000 to 110,000
Self-Help	40,000 to 90,000
Standard Nonfiction	70,000 to 80,000

Can I edit my own book?

Is the real question here *can* you? Or *should* you? Our answer to this is a very strong caution to not edit your own book—even if you're an editor. Have people done it? Absolutely. Have they done it well? Sure. Then why shouldn't *you* edit your own book? Because the human mind has a wonderful capacity to fill in the blanks and correct mistakes in your own work without always telling you it's doing it and you will miss the errors.

And it's not all about obvious grammar and typos. Editors do content editing, too. You will invariably skip over plot holes because you remember the plot you thought about even if you didn't actually write it. You will not catch that you accidentally changed the color of your character's hair from black to brown halfway through the book because you see the character in your mind, and even when you read "brown," you still see "black."

The Amazon bookstore is filled with wonderful stories that will never make it anywhere because the quality is just not up to the standard of most readers. People want a good product when they buy something, even if it's free. The expectation for quality is even higher if you intend to pitch your story to a traditional publisher. Even if you know they'll edit the story if they choose to publish it, realize that they still don't want to work harder to read a story that hasn't been properly edited. **Don't give editors, agents, or publishers an easy reason to reject your work.** They see so many manuscripts that a bad edit is often the first thing that sends the story to the "rejected" pile. So, do yourself a favor and have your story professionally edited before you decide to self-publish or pitch it to an agent or publisher.

How do I know if my book is good?

Good question! "Good" is a very subjective word. One person's "good" is another person's "bad." Don't worry about whether the story is good. Just focus on telling it. If it inspires you, that's good enough.

How do I create a writing schedule?

No single schedule works for every writer. But we've put together what we think is the next best thing. Check out the chapter entitled *Writing Starts with an Ugly First Draft* to read how you can build a writing habit, and then check out *Part II* to see a great example of a writing schedule. Between these two sections, you can build a great writing schedule that works specifically for you.

How do I know my story is finished?

There are different thresholds of "finished" when you're a writer. Some writers consider their story finished when they write the last word of their first draft and type those glorious words, "The End." Others say their story is finished when they turn in the last edits to the editor. And still others will only call it finished when their story is finally published. In reality, each of those points is a version of finished, and they should all be celebrated. It's a lot of work to write a story, and you should be proud of each step you take to bring your story to life.

How do I know my story is original?

If it's your idea and it's in your own words, it's original. We could give a thousand writers an identical writing prompt, and no two writers will ever write the story exactly the same. Sure, some might come out sounding similar, but each story will have words, phrases, and ideas unique to the writer.

Where do I start?

Well, you made a great start when you picked up the ***Inkslinger – 99-Day Guided Writing Experience***! Now, it's all about taking the first piece of advice we gave you in the introduction: **just start writing!** Don't worry about formatting or making it perfect. Just write the story. If you read this book and keep on writing, you'll know what to do from there.

Target Audience

Let's face it, it's every author's dream to write a best seller. Wouldn't it be awesome to write a book that gets featured prominently in every bookstore window and hangs around for weeks and months, or even years, on the major literary lists? Oh, to be the author of a featured book that's picked for all the book clubs and one that gets hawked by A-list celebrities on their talk shows. Can you imagine writing a book that becomes standard reading for all colleges or high schools?

That would be really something! In fact, we know a great little how-to book about writing that would change some lives. (Hint: it's this one!) But back to the target audience thing.

Not everything is going to appeal to everybody. So, it makes more sense to write about something you're interested in with a specific audience in mind. This will provide clarity to your work and make the writing tighter. Good, focused work will appeal to a lot more people than anything that is overly generalized.

Take *To Kill a Mockingbird*. The author, Harper Lee, never expected her book to be successful. In fact, when she turned it in for publication, she "…was hoping for a quick and merciful death at the hands of reviewers…" To her surprise, the book has never been out of print since its publication in 1960 and has been a standard text in classrooms for more than half a century.

Harper Lee wrote what she knew. The story is loosely based on her childhood and hometown with a fictionalized plot. Prior to writing *To Kill a Mockingbird*, she'd only published a few articles and short stories focused on racial injustice—a topic that was not written about very often during that time.

Her target audience was people like her: people who came of age in the 1940s and 50s, from the South, middle class, educated, interested in racial injustice. That's who she expected would read her book. Unfortunately, that was not a huge demographic in those days. But her book resonated so deeply with that set of people that they wouldn't stop talking about it, which generated interest, and the popularity rapidly grew from there.

That particular success story does not work in reverse. It just wouldn't be the same book if Harper Lee had tried to make it resonate with everyone. The power of the message in the book would have been diminished, or maybe even the opposite of what she wanted to say, given the attitudes toward race at the time of the book's publication.

This underscores the need to understand your target audience when you're writing your story.

Who do *you* want to read *your* work?

Do you have a children's book in mind? Or maybe it's an adult book. There are huge markets that target the middle area of Young Adult and Tween books, too. But, beyond that, there are audiences within audiences. For example, female, adults, born during the 1980s, who read romances about werewolves, with no graphic sex or violence. That's a real thing.

Defining your target audience is important because you want to make sure that you are using the language, imagery, and story details that will resonate with your particular audience while writing your manuscript.

Some writers know their target audience before they start writing. Others discover their target audience after they have written the story. The main thing is it's important to know who it is so you can tailor the story to fit the audience you want it to appeal to.

A simple way to define your target audience is to develop a profile of the people you think would be most likely to read your work. Start by answering these questions:

- What kind of story, or genre, are you writing? (Genres often come with specific audiences already identified.)
- Why are you writing this particular story?
- What message do you want your story to impart?
- Which audience will the message or theme best suit?

Once you've answered those questions, try to determine some details about your target audience:

- Demographics
  - Age
  - Geography
  - Gender
  - Income level
  - Education level
  - Marital or family status
  - Occupation
  - Cultural or ethnic background

- Individual Personal Details
  - Personality
  - Attitudes
  - Values
  - Interests/hobbies
  - Lifestyle
  - Behavior

- Digging Deeper
    - What sets my target audience apart from others?
    - Does my target audience specifically like/dislike certain things?
    - Is there a certain content that is more or less appropriate for my audience?
    - What tone/voice/language is appropriate for my target audience?

You may answer these questions and find a new audience for the kind of writing you like to do. That's actually pretty cool. That gives you an opportunity to attract that audience and give them the book they've been waiting for all their lives. That's a great way to build a loyal fan base.

The main benefit of identifying your target audience is that it allows you to focus on the thing you want to write about, which will help tighten your writing so it will resonate for the people you want it to resonate with.

Genre

A genre is a way to describe the category of literature in which an author writes. In broad terms, there are two types of literature:

Nonfiction – writing that is based on fact

Fiction – stories depicting imaginary events and people

Within these two types of literature, there are numerous genres, which continue to expand as writers explore new ways to create. Within nonfiction are genres such as biography, memoir, textbook, and self-help, among others. Fiction consists of genres such as romance, science fiction, horror, thriller, humor, fantasy, among others. Check out the Genre topic in Wikipedia to see the ever-changing lists.

Generally, most writers tend to lean toward a certain genre in their work, and the writer and their genre become a brand. But as it has become easier to search for books in the digital age, it has become more common for writers to explore multiple genres. Not long ago, when most books were purchased or loaned out from brick and mortar buildings, writers were strongly persuaded to work within a single genre because the books were organized physically on shelves, either by genre, author name, or sometimes topic. This made it necessary for an author to decide how they wanted to be classified, and usually they chose the way that would make it easier for a reader to discover their books or find them if they knew exactly what they were looking for. Now, in this computerized world, where books are mostly purchased online or provided in electronic format, collections can be cross-referenced in many ways, so a writer is not as constrained by a genre-specific brand.

While it is increasingly common for writers to work in multiple genres, it's still beneficial for a writer to categorize their individual works in specific genres. This helps readers to find them, and it lets readers know what to expect when they pick up additional works by the same author. It's frustrating for a reader to fall in love with an author's work in one genre, only to pick up a new book and find that it is completely different. Can you imagine reading Stephen King horror books for years only to pick up a new one to discover it's a historical romance without… gasp… anyone being savagely murdered by a preternatural being? All but a few very well-read people would have something to say about that!

Finally, if you do decide to branch out, just understand that confusion could ensue, so take measures to make sure your readers can tell what the book is about. After you read the rest of this guide, you will surely have many ideas on how to do that.

Text Elements: Fiction

The following subjects cover a few areas we consider to be important when writing fiction, but that doesn't mean they're confined solely to fiction. For instance point of view is important to both fiction and nonfiction, but nonfiction genres tend to gravitate to particular points of views. We've included these topics in the fiction section because they have more of an affect fiction writing.

Regardless of whether you're writing fiction or nonfiction, give this section a read.

Story Arc and Plot

The plot is made up of the individual events of a story and the story arc is the sequence of events in which the story unfolds. While the plot is what the story is *about*, the arc is the way the plot is *structured*. Some people may refer to the story arc as the Three-Act or the Five-Act Structure, which are the most frequently used structures, but there are other ways in which to structure your story. For the purpose of this guide, we'll focus on the Three-Act and Five-Act structures.

The number of acts is a holdover from a time when stories would be acted out as plays, and each act was roughly the same length and focused on how the specific components of the story were performed. For instance, the Three-Act structure is laid out in the following manner: Act 1 – the set up; Act 2 – the confrontation; Act 3 – the crisis/climax. Others may express this as the beginning, the middle, and the end. The Five-Act structure is similar to the Three-Act structure with a little more detail thrown in: Act 1 – the setup; Act 2 – rising action, where the conflicts begin; Act 3 – climax; Act 4 – falling action, where all of the plot points are tied up; and Act 5 – the resolution.

Is structure important? Yes. Are there stories that don't follow a structure? Yes, but they are few and far between, and readers are used to structured stories, so we strongly suggest the use of one of these two structures, unless you have another structure in mind.

Which one should you choose? It's a personal choice. The Three-Act structure is simpler, so it might be easier to start with if you're a new writer, but the Five-Act structure provides additional guidance on building tension and tying up plot points.

Number of acts aside, the traditional story is about the transformation of the main character(s). The arc is the journey of the character toward the change. The arc is important because each of the elements builds upon the last, working together in a delicate balance, creating tension, evoking emotion, and creating a framework that captivates the reader until the very end.

The classic arc, devised by a 19th century playwright named Gustav Freytag, has five core elements (not to be confused with the number of acts). They are:

Exposition – The introduction of the story to the reader, it provides some information for the reader, so they get a sense of what the story is about, which should hook them, contain some background information, introduce the main characters, and it sets the tone for the story. A major event in the exposition should be the inciting incident.

> **Inciting Incident** – The inciting incident happens near the start of the story, usually within the first several pages, and tells the reader what the story is about. The incident disturbs the routine and expectations of the main characters and propels the story forward while the character deals with the incident and its repercussions.

Rising Action – This usually starts with, or right after, the inciting incident, which is the trigger that sets the story into motion. The writer devises a series of plot points, each adding to the next, increasing the tension, until the crisis comes to a head, resulting in the next element…

Climax – This is where much of the excitement happens, the part where the tension breaks, the story hits its turning point, and a solution is revealed. This is the point where the main character's moment of truth occurs, when a decision is made.

Falling Action – This is where the reader learns the consequences of the main character's actions surrounding the major conflict and where the loose ends start to get tied up.

Resolution – Also known as the denouement, the resolution is how the story ends, closing all the sub-plots and putting final closure on the loop of the story. This is where we see how the main character and the world around them have changed.

Believe it or not, even readers who are the least versed in literary knowledge can tell when a story arc is missing one of these critical elements. Even children's books use them. The reader can become bored if the expected tension is missing. Bad reviews on Goodreads will be had if a story line ends without resolution. And folks can become quite angry if the romance they're reading doesn't have a happy ending or the bad guy in the thriller doesn't get what's coming to them. Story arcs come with expectations. And while those expectations can be stretched or changed in some creative ways, unless you know what is expected, it is quite difficult to pull off the unexpected in a successful way.

Point of View (POV)

Point of View is simple: who's telling the story?

We say POV is simple, but it's actually an aspect of writing that writers struggle with most. Who tells the story can have a major impact on the way the story is delivered. Not only does it set a certain tone and cadence for a story, it can introduce different opportunities or difficulties in *what* information can be given and *when* it can be given.

The person telling the story is called the narrator, and the narrator can be anyone who has knowledge of the sequence of events that occur during the telling of the story. The narrator plays a pivotal role because what knowledge they have, what they say, and how they say it make the story unique and compelling. The narrator's *perspective* is also an important aspect of POV. What kind of access do they have to the details of the story? Are they in the minds of the characters? Or are they standing across the street watching them?

Choosing the narrator will set the tone and the pace of the story more than any other element, so take care when selecting your narrator to ensure their perspective will be effective through every twist and turn of your story.

There are three basic points of view:

First Person

First Person is easy to identify because the story is related using I, me, and myself. It's usually a person telling a story as it is happening or as they remember it. It can be a main character or a secondary character reciting the story, providing a first-hand account of what is or has happened to and around them as the story unfolds.

First person often gives a personal *voice* to the story, imbuing it with the personality of the narrator, providing a way to convey emotions in a way that is organic to the story without too much description or exposition. The perspective of the narrator can also add interesting elements, or withhold critical information to the plot, depending on the narrator's knowledge of what is happening.

Second Person

One of the least common points of view, Second Person is identified by its use of the words you, your, and yourself. It isn't used very often in fiction because it can come off as awkward; however, it can be found in how-to books, where a narrator instructs the reader, and in humor books, where the narrator might be a character telling a long joke. This guide is an example of Second Person.

Third Person

Third Person is probably the most versatile point of view, allowing the writer to take advantage of an almost infinite array of methods to tell the story. It can be used to give the reader a very wide view of what is happening in the story, or it can provide a very narrow view, allowing the writer to reveal plot points when and how they want them revealed.

There are a few ways to use Third Person point of view:

Third Person Omniscient

In this point of view, the narrator knows everything about what is happening in the story, to every character, internally and externally, and at all times. They know everything that has happened in the past, the present, the future, and possibly even in alternative realities- the "could-have-beens."

Third Person Multiple

In this point of view, the story is told from the

perspective of more than one character. The writer accomplishes this by switching the POV from person to person, using the unique views as opportunities to relay information as it is being seen from the various characters.

One thing to be careful about is something called "head-hopping." Head-hopping is when a writer changes the point of view from one character to another in the same scene, often without a graceful transition. This can be very confusing to the reader as they try to figure out who is thinking what.

While most writers say to avoid head-hopping all together, some writers enjoy using it, especially when they're trying to evoke a certain powerful emotional tension in a scene. No matter the preference, a writer must ensure that it is obvious who is telling the story at any given moment. This can be accomplished by making it obvious who is thinking or speaking at all times.

Third Person Limited

This point of view, popular in thriller and crime novels, tells the story from the POV of a single character in the story, revealing things about other characters only in a way related to that one character. This method of POV provides the writer with a way to build tension by holding on to certain information until a critical point in the story. It can be used effectively in other genres and is considered the most flexible of POVs, because the writer is able to manipulate the information conveyed in the most believable fashion.

When selecting a POV, just know that **consistency is key**. Once you've selected it, it's important to stick with what you've selected. Otherwise, you'll confuse your reader.

A word about tense: Tense is how a writer conveys *when* the actions in a story are happening: **past, present, or future**. To make things more complicated, in English, there are also *simple* and *perfect* tenses for past, present, and future, which we won't get into here because we want to keep this simple (and we don't want to bring back bad memories of high school English classes.)

The important take-away here is that most novels use *third person, past tense*. While not specific to Point of View, the use of tense in a novel is one of the things that trips new writers up. So, once again, what you want to do is to pick a tense and stick to it. Most readers prefer to have a story told in a uniform tense, otherwise they have to work at keeping track of the action in the story, and readers generally don't want to work. They want to be swept away.

Outline - Fiction

Each writer has a different process. Some writers need to have a detailed plot outline before they start, and some just start writing and play it by the seat of their pants. Simply put, you're either a Plotter or a Pantser. Or somewhere in between—a Plantster. Clear as mud, huh?

The thing is, you probably know who you are. And if you don't, that's okay. You'll figure it out. Our recommendation is to go with what you feel most comfortable with, and if you don't have an idea, start as a Plotter and you'll know pretty quickly if you'd rather be a Pantser.

Regardless of what way you lean, it's always a good idea to know the basic plot details you want to have in your story to get started. This gives you a focus and keeps you moving forward. If you don't have a basic idea and just figure you'll make it up as you go along, you risk getting stuck, or worse, you may even write yourself into a corner and have to backtrack by rewriting some of the story just to get to the next chapter. Also, after you have written a certain number of words, it doesn't matter what kind of memory you have☐you'll probably forget some of what you've written. That's when plot holes happen. So, even if you're a Pantser, you may want to keep a log of major details to make sure you close out plot points you've started.

Start with the broad strokes and build in the detail as you go along.

We recommend starting with an outline of the main components of the classic arc (see *Story Arc*). What are the exposition, rising action, climax, falling action, and resolution?

> **An Example:** A middle class kid in Indiana gets a dog after his mother dies **(exposition)**. The kid's dad remarries **(inciting incident)**, and the kid acts out **(rising action)**, finally running away. The dog becomes a hero by saving the kid in a fire but dies in doing so **(climax)**. The kid grieves but learns that love doesn't die when you lose someone **(falling action)**. The kid decides to give his stepmother a chance, and the kid stops acting up, goes to college, and becomes a famous dog trainer **(resolution)**.

Once the broad strokes are established, some writers may want to go into more detail about the story in a chapter-by-chapter or scene-by-scene outline, planning out each beat of the story.

Story beats are the sequence of events that make up a story through specific points where a writer shifts the tone in a deliberate way to control the tension through the emotional journey of their characters. While every story is unique, certain genres rely on the same general beat sequences. For example, one popular set of beats are called the Hero's Journey, which was adapted by Christopher Vogler and can be seen in epic fiction. There are also general romance beats, horror beats, etc. We won't go into detail about the general beats for each genre, but it's a good thing for a writer to know the beats of the genre they write in.

Here's a basic outline example in chapter form:

> Ch 1 – Boy is at his mother's funeral with his dad **(opening hook)**, boy refuses to cry
>
> Ch 2 – Boy gets ready for bed after the funeral and hears his father crying, doesn't know what to do **(exposition)**
>
> Ch 3 – Boy's father is worried about son's inability to cry, talks to boy, boy brushes it off **(exposition)**
>
> Ch 4 – Boy and father start to learn how to manage without mother, father gets boy a puppy **(exposition)**
>
> Ch 5 – Father meets someone **(inciting incident)**, boy is upset, falls to sleep with dog on dog's bed
>
> Ch 6 – Boy starts to fail school, loses friends, his dog is his only friend **(rising action)**

Ch 7 – Father marries new woman

Ch 8 – Boy runs away with dog, destination is a vacation spot the family went to when mom was alive (**rising action**)

Ch 9 – Dog protects boy from strangers on their journey (**rising action**)

Ch 10 – Boy gets to vacation house, breaks in, it's cold, starts fire in fireplace, accidentally catches house on fire, dog gets boy out, but dog dies from injuries (**climax**)

Ch 11 – Etc.

You get the idea. The outline is your guide. You can even label certain parts with the components of the classic arc to make sure you've included them in your story. What you put into it should be useful to you to remember key details and to plan the flow of the story. Put in as much detail or as little detail as you want. Just because you include something in the outline doesn't mean you have to include it in the story. If you start writing the story and you decide to change something it's okay. Just update the outline and go back to your story.

Feel free to write our example story if you're looking for ideas. It's a classic storyline, but every author is unique and will tell it differently.

Setting

Setting is one of the more critical elements of a story. Some would call it the backdrop to your book, or the sensory aspects of the story, but setting is so much more than the descriptive imagery of sight, smell, taste, sound, and touch. Setting is an opportunity to immerse the reader in the story.

Setting can affect the mood, impart meaning, and set expectations for the reader in ways other than stating them directly. The best stories are often the ones using setting to evoke emotions by layering multiple senses through setting the scene.

Consider the following examples. Both passages convey a character's escape through the forest. The first gets the point across, but the second uses the setting to impart the character's challenges more effectively, thus evoking heightened emotion from the reader.

Example:

> Henry escaped through the forest, dodging this way and that to avoid the many obstacles in his way. At one point, he had to cross a wide river, which was good because the dogs were on his trail and he needed to throw them off his scent.

Versus:

> The dense undergrowth and forest canopy blocked the moonlight, providing visual protection for Henry, but his legs were weary as he skirted a boulder and leapt over yet another fallen tree in his attempts to evade capture. Cresting a hill and tumbling down a steep embankment, he nearly fell head-first into the swollen river. It took him several attempts to find a way across. By now, his pace was barely at a slow jog and he held his side against a stabbing pain, but by the fading sounds of pursuit, he dared to hope he'd finally thrown the baying dogs off his scent.

The major aspects of setting are:

- **Location** – The physical location where the story takes place.
- **Period** – Well-known periods in human history.
- **Time** – The time of day the scene is taking place.

- **Physical environment** – Can be the geography or atmosphere, such as lighting, temperature, weather, etc.
- **Mood** – Mood can be conveyed by smells, colors, textures, temperatures, lighting, and other sensory elements.
- **Architecture and design** – Building descriptions and decoration.
- **Historical events** – Especially if the historic events are well-known.
- **Culturally significant objects or events** – Holidays, traditions, and symbols evoke entire sets of expectations.
- **Sounds** – Another sensory aspect, descriptions of sound can provide a vast set of details to a reader.

If done correctly, describing the setting can convey more than what is specifically written just by choosing the right elements to include in it. For instance, in the above example, merely mentioning moonlight instantly creates a specific scene in the reader's mind much different than if the writer had said it was daytime. This makes for a richer, multi-dimensional experience for the reader, where their personal thoughts and feelings about being chased through a forest at night will fill in additional details that the writer doesn't even need to mention.

In short, when you think about where your story takes place, you're only beginning to describe it if you merely tell the reader where the character's feet may be standing.

Character Sketches

When asked how they come up with their characters, writers often say that the characters write themselves. While it can feel like that, and it sounds so romantic and mystical to describe it like that, we all know it isn't true. The writer is in control of every character they put in their stories. When it feels like the characters are writing themselves, it means that you're doing a great job of writing them.

Character development is often one of the most overlooked parts of writing a story. In order to write a compelling story, the characters must have real depth to be truly believable. You can skimp on many things, but this is not one of them. If you're going to spend time on any one thing, spend it on character development.

Take some time to get to know your characters. Go beyond the things that happen to them in your story and figure out as much about them as you can. Start with the basics, such as physical description, and go from there. Figure out their personalities, their motivations, their desires, and their fears. Do they have families? Do they get along with their parents? Do they nurture deep friendships, or do they hold people at arm's length? Why? Are they the type to walk by a person asking for money on the street? Or do they give them the money? Do they have pets? Phobias? Wild aspirations? What's their favorite flavor of Skittles? Coffee or tea? Omnivore, carnivore, or vegivore? (That's a real word! Who knew?)

Many of the things you know about your characters may never even make it into the book, but if you know enough about them, you can insert nuanced behaviors that will make you a show, not tell, author. (See more about *Show, Don't Tell* later.)

Character sketches are more complex for the main characters, are moderately complex for secondary characters, and become simpler the less important the character is to the story. If a character is just a name mentioned in passing, you may want to consider whether they really need to be a part of the story at all. The rule of thumb in whether a character should be included in the story is whether they move the plot along. If the story is just as strong without a character in it, it is a good sign that the character isn't necessary. Almost every author has or will experience the pain of cutting out a character they have come to love but who does nothing to advance the plot. If you're not sure, write the character into the scene. You can always edit them out during revisions.

Who knows? Creativity is an unpredictable thing. Maybe a character who starts out as a side character twice removed will evolve through the course of the story into a key player. But when in doubt, write it out!

When you begin a character sketch, start with the aspects most relevant to the story and work deeper. Some details will only become apparent during the writing of the story, and you'll choose to add to the sketches as they come to you. For instance, it may become a necessary plot point to give a character a sibling. This sibling might merely be mentioned, or they could play a more important part of the story. Based on the character's importance to the story, you can make an in-depth sketch or a simple one. This is your call.

Below are some of the items you may want to include in a character sketch:

- Name
- Age
- Physical traits (hair/eye color, height, scars, tattoos, dress, etc.)
- General character traits (habits/quirks, demeanor, how people regard them, etc.)
- Psychological traits (how they think, what mental strengths/weaknesses drive them, etc.)
- Motivation/desires/fears
- Strengths/virtues
- Weaknesses/faults
- Behavior

- Relationships
- Background
- What is their role in the story?
- How do they propel the story forward?
- Do they change through the story line?
- Any other relevant details?

Again, not all the details you sketch out will make it directly into your story, but all of them will contribute to the way the character thinks and behaves throughout the story. For example, a character sketch may have details of a troubled youth, but the character's past is not included in the story you are telling. However, it can affect the way the character relates to other characters.

The main idea here is to create rich characters readers can connect with. If the reader connects with the characters, they will almost always like the story.

Conflict

Conflict is the single most important thing in a story. Without conflict, a story does not exist. It is just a bunch of words strung together in a haphazard way that may describe random things, sometimes contain beautiful imagery, and may even entertain people to a certain extent, but it isn't a story unless there is point to it—which is essentially what the conflict is. Does the protagonist achieve what they originally set out to do, even if they didn't know they were signed up to do something in the first place?

A number of different kinds of conflict can occur in a story. We'll explore some of the more common literary conflicts below. But before we do that, let's talk about the difference between Internal and External conflicts.

> **Internal Conflict** – Internal conflict is when a character faces challenges or struggles that occur within the character's mind, heart, or soul. The protagonist

may be presented with a difficult psychological journey, a heart wrenching choice, a confrontation that poses a moral dilemma, or something that puts their beliefs to a test. They may discuss or seek advice on the issues with other characters or as they narrate the story, but ultimately the character needs to come to a personal decision by the end of the story.

External Conflict – External conflicts are challenges that come from a source outside the character's control. Something out of their control comes between the character's desires or motivations, making it difficult for the character to obtain what they are looking for. Often, it is the character's responses to the issues arising from the conflict that raise tension and bring on the culmination or climax.

Can a good story have both internal and external conflicts? Absolutely. Expressing both in the main plot, or as a subplot, can provide a wonderful richness to the story. Which leads us to some of the more familiar literary conflicts.

Character versus Self – As noted above, this is when the character wrestles with themselves over a choice, a moral reckoning, or a set of desires that may lead to different outcomes. This will almost always be depicted as an *internal conflict*. All other conflicts consist of external forces, presented by outside forces as described in the following conflicts.

Character versus Character – This one is pretty

obvious. Two characters have needs that are opposed to one another's. It could be a simple love/hate relationship, a difference of opinion, or any number of situations that can lead up to a culminating scene where one triumphs over the other, concedes to the other, or they come to a compromise.

Character versus Nature – Nature can provide many kinds of conflict, from the very simple to the very challenging. A character can weave a nice plot or sub-plot about their frustrations about weeds in their garden, or it can get really intense with something like a family fleeing a forest fire, a rabid grizzly, or an approaching comet.

Character versus Supernatural – A very popular conflict in literature recently is the use of the supernatural, such as vampires, ghosts, demons, and the like. Many times, this kind of conflict will contain elements of the other literary conflicts in tandem with the primary conflict.

Character versus Society – Character versus society is when a character is left to overcome struggles between them and societal structures. It can be a conflict with the government, cultural norms, religious tensions, moral systems, changes in technology, or maybe it's a simple disagreement between local townspeople, which can be pretty awful, too. In most instances of Character versus Society, the conflict is one of right versus wrong or a desire or aversion to evolving traditional or stagnant views. Many times, this conflict will have far-reaching impacts beyond the specific situation at hand.

There are other literary conflicts, too. And as you plan your story, you may find you're writing a conflict slightly different to something we just covered, but the principals are very similar.

Conflict is the main tool used to propel a story forward through gradually rising tension until the conflict comes to a reckoning point. It creates a dynamic way to engage the reader, keeping them invested in the story to discover how the plotline resolves. Interestingly enough, most genres have expected ways to address the conflict. In romance, the reader expects a happy ending. In action, the reader expects the good side to win. In horror and thrillers, the villain is defeated. But this is not always the case. What *is* always the case is that conflicts are resolved with a major final action that satisfies the reader, while others are manufactured to come to a resolution that causes the reader to think about the deeper meaning imparted by the story. Some may argue that a good book does both. It really depends on the intention of the author and the preferences of the reader.

The main takeaways here are that all plotlines require a primary conflict to guide the story, and knowing what that conflict is will help you ground your book into a focused journey toward a satisfying resolution for both you and the reader.

Rising Action and Creating Tension

The rising action of a story consists of a series of events or plot points that build the story's tension, leading up to the climax. A major portion of the plotline, rising action is where the main conflict is presented and all the minor conflicts the characters go through to in order to get to a resolution.

Previously, in the chapter called *Conflict*, we talked about what conflict is. We explained that conflict *is* the story. It's the reason the main characters are doing what they're doing. The reader commits to the story to find out how the writer resolves the conflict. They want to know *why* the character is conflicted as much as they want to know *what* the character does to resolve the conflict. Here, we will tell you effective ways to introduce the conflicts through the story's rising action.

The rising action is meant to engage the reader and invest them in the outcome. This section of the story explains the character's motivations and desires and what blocks the characters from obtaining them. This also creates uncertainty that things may not go as expected, and the tension builds as the story progresses, resulting in the climax which is the most dramatic point of the story.

Each plot point in the rising action should help build and develop the story's primary conflict. Along with the primary conflict, minor conflicts may also come into play. Some of them may support the development of the major conflict, and some may run parallel to the main conflict, and some may be red herrings to the main conflict. However, each conflict should have a believable purpose in the story, helping to move it forward toward the resolution.

There are no hard rules for how long the rising action must play out, but tension should increase as the rising action goes on. This does not mean that every scene must become a bigger and bigger production, although that can be one way to increase tension. It means that the reader's suspense should build until they can no longer wait to find out what happens. This is called the scene and sequel pattern. Scenes, in written form, can be viewed as a unit of conflict, where the characters are moving forward toward their desired goals. A sequel is the transition linking one scene to another, and it is in this transition where a character has a reaction, considers the situation, and reaches a decision, thus moving the story forward and either builds or releases tension. In this technique, the writer deliberately relates the procession of scenes so that they are not isolated snippets of activity, but interconnected actions and reactions that ultimately propel the characters to the story's climax. The tension can go up and down or steadily increase. Creating this tension is an art form.

The Climax

You've been writing a story, weaving together a world consisting of events and interesting characters, and you're finally at the point where it all comes together in a major event. Each detail you've painstakingly created makes sense now, and the reader knows why the characters have been doing what they've been doing and what it is they have to do to resolve all the conflicts they have been subjected to or have instigated.

This is the climax of the story, where the reader finally knows the outcome of the main conflict.

Simply put, the climax is the part of the story, near the end, where all the buildup culminates in the story's final turning point. All that comes later is simply the falling action, where all the minor story lines get tied up and resolved.

The art of creating a successful climax happens in the rising action, which we discussed in the previous section. Building

tension, providing a rich plotline, and establishing a compelling conflict result in a satisfying climax.

The Falling Action

The falling action is the part of the plot following the climax, where the tension has abated, and all the situations the characters have been through are addressed, right before the conclusion, or resolution. The falling action can sometimes become blurred with the resolution, which is the very end of the story, but the falling action is more about what lessons the characters have learned on their journey through the story than it is about the story's ending.

The falling action begins with the climax, where the primary conflict is explained and addressed. During this section of the story, the tension releases, the writer ties up loose strings, and the reader finally has answers to all questions that may have come up through the storytelling.

Resolution, Also Fancily Known as the Denouement

The resolution is pretty much what it sounds like: the end of the book, when all the plot points get fully resolved.

There's another word commonly used for it because writers are a pretentious bunch (we can say that because we are writers and we know), and that is the denouement. It's a French word that means to untie, so you can look at the denouement as the place where all the strategic knots the author has placed throughout the story become un-knotted and the reader gets to relax.

Have you ever read a book where an author leaves things hanging? We're not talking about a cliff-hanger ending, where you know a sequel will help close out questions left at the end of the previous book. It can be a big plot point or a small detail, but when a reader is left wondering what happened, it's generally not a good thing. The reader isn't likely to recommend the book or read other books by an author if they are left feeling frustrated by how the author closes out the story.

The falling action is where all the hanging questions, mysteries, and unexplained plot points get resolved. This is as true for nonfiction as it is for fiction. We know that real life isn't always neat and tidy, but even the events of a biography need closure. Even a simple acknowledgement from the author about the lack of closure and what it has caused relative to the events depicted in the narrative is a closure of sorts.

The questions can be obvious, such as major plot points like "Who done it?" or why a character did a particular thing. Or they can be small things like a barking dog or a mysterious letter that was never explained.

Don't get the denouement confused with an epilogue, though. An epilogue is more about giving a glimpse at the characters' futures after their exciting adventure.

Text Elements: Nonfiction

Now that we've talked your ear off about the fiction side of writing, let's take a little time to go over the nonfiction side of writing. After all, recent statistics reveal that three out of every five books published are nonfiction.

While the one compelling difference setting nonfiction apart from fiction is the true versus imaginary characters and events thing, nonfiction books can differ from fiction in other ways. In most cases, nonfiction does not contain setting, descriptive imagery, figurative language, plot, or characterization. This is not always the case, of course, as you may see some of the elements we've gone over in memoirs or biographies, but these are some areas where you might run into some key structural differences in the two types of literature.

We don't go into detail about the different nonfiction genres, because each of those are enough to fill an entire book on their own, but we will briefly describe some of the basic elements of nonfiction in the following sections.

Types of Nonfiction

Most nonfiction serves to fulfil one of the following three purposes: to inform; to make an argument (persuade); and to tell a story. Within each of these three areas, there are different types of writing that can be used to present the topic. We won't go into the specifics on how to organize each of the types, but we will explain what they are and some of the genres they might suit.

- **Inform**
    - ○ **Expository** – the purpose of this kind of writing is to expose, explain or inform about a topic. Usually, there is a thesis statement or an objective stated in the beginning and the body of the writing provides supporting information to the thesis, and it is all summed up in the end. This type of writing is used quite a bit in academia, essays, journalism, and descriptive instruction manuals.

- **Instructional** – is a type of writing presented in a set-by-step format. Often it is presented in a direct, short and sweet, way with active voice and a simple writing style. It may be accompanied with illustrations, and may be broken into sub-processes to aid in the absorption of the material being presented. How-to books, manuals, and text books are often written this way.
- **Reference** – is a collection of specifically arranged, short descriptions of various topics, containing just enough information to guide a reader toward an information source with more in-depth detail. Examples of reference work are dictionaries, encyclopedias, almanacs, etc.
- **Journalism** – is the way in which writers prepare news stories for broadcast via newspapers, magazines, and websites. The most popular structure for this is called the inverted pyramid. This is when the information is presented in a descending order of importance, with the most important information, or the lead, first and the remaining body of the story supports the lead.

- **Make an argument, or to persuade**
  - **Persuasive** – this type of writing is when a writer takes a position on a topic and tries to

sway the reader, using appeals to logic, ethics, and emotions. Often, this type of writing makes use of emotional language, rhetoric, and an appeal to personal connection. You may see persuasive writing in essays and articles.

- **Tell a story**
  - **Narrative** – tells a true story, usually in a chronological sequence of related events about a person, event, or place. This type of writing may rely on setting, characterization, an inciting event, and other aspects of fiction writing in order to tell a compelling but factual story. This kind of writing can be found in memoirs, literary journalism, biographies, and nonfiction short stories.
  - **Descriptive** – this writing style is used when a writer wants to convey a detailed and immersive true experience using the five senses. More often found in fiction, it can also be found in some nonfiction work such as travel guides, memoirs, biographies, and first-hand accounts of events.

Nonfiction Text Structures

Text structure is the way a book is organized, and the organization of a book can be an important factor influencing the reader's successful connection to and absorption of the material. Providing the information in a way that aids in reader comprehension is critical and picking the right structure depends largely on the target audience and the topic.

We've chosen to focus on what we consider the five primary nonfiction text structures and the genres they best support.

- **Description** – this structure uses the descriptive writing style we touched on above. This structure relies on a detailed description, often relying on a story format to provide a immersive experience for the reader. Often, this structure provides a lot of information and it's up to the reader to determine what information they think is important and what information they can skim through. Readers who enjoy this kind of structure are often people who are imaginative and like to build detailed events in their minds. This type of structure may be difficult for people who rely on memorization to remember what they read. Some genres that work well with this structure are memoirs, biographies, and travel guides.

- **Sequence** – work presented in an order of chronological events. This might be used in how-to books, memoirs, history books, and biographies.
- **Cause and Effect** – this structure is used to illustrate how one or more events caused or had an effect on succeeding events. The cause and effect could be a single instance of one event affecting another, or it can be a succession of events causing impact to later events. You might see this in history books.
- **Compare and Contrast** – is a structure that lends itself to demonstrating how two or more things are the same or different. Many children's' books use this structure as does educational literature.
- **Problem and Solution** – a structure that presents a problem, why it needs to be fixed, and finally provides a solution. This can be used in a very direct way, such as instructional manuals and how-to books, but it can also be an effective structure in educational material and as way to present the main point in a memoir or biography.

It's important to keep in mind that some texts may use more

than one kind of structure in a single work. For example, a memoir is typically going to be written in a descriptive structure, but will most likely also portray the content in a chronological order.

In addition to understanding the types of nonfiction structure, it's important to craft your work around a solid physical structure. Much like the story arc we discussed in the fiction section, nonfiction work requires a framework in which to mold your work around. For nonfiction, it's a little simpler. We start with the beginning, the middle, and the end and add the other elements depending on the needs of the genre and the topic.

Before you even start writing, make sure you know what the topic is, or how you intend to solve a problem, and how you plan to summarize it. Once you have a central idea, you can flesh it out from there. A clearly defined premise is critical for you to develop a strong supporting body of information, keep the reader engaged, and for you to stay on topic and resist tangents. You don't necessarily need to have the entire book planned out before you start writing, but you do need to know if you have enough material to write an entire book.

The Beginning

Regardless of the topic, writing style, or structure of the work, the reader needs to know what the book is about and what they can expect to get from reading it. This is presented at the start, by clearly stating why you're writing the book. Unlike most fictional work, where you want to preserve some element of surprise toward the end, in nonfiction you usually want to be upfront about what happens at the end before you even get started. Whether it's literally to solve a specific problem, convey a message, inform the reader about something, or to teach a lesson, you need to do the set up. For books telling a story, such as a memoir, what sets the story in motion? What is the inciting incident? Why is the story important to tell? For how-to, or instructional books, what's the problem you plan to solve? For either kind of book, what kind of person wants to read it? Why are you the right person to write it? This leads us to an important question:

What's your angle?

What makes this story unique to you? Are there other books already written about the subject? If so, what makes your book different than the others? If you're writing a memoir, what will the reader get out of it that they won't get out of all the other memoirs? If you're solving a problem, what makes you an expert at it? If you can't tell the reader why they want to read your book, you might have a hard time writing a compelling book.

The Middle

The middle is where you provide the steps or information

the reader wants to know about the subject. You'll be working toward a defined objective and all work here should support that objective. What are the major steps or events you want to include to propel the instruction or story forward? Does the information you provide directly support the journey toward a solution or the events that lead up to a satisfying conclusion for the reader? If you are writing an instructional book, you'll want to offer creative ideas and include a plan of action to support the proposed solution. This makes it extremely important to:

Do Your Research

By definition nonfiction is based in fact. Whether you're writing a memoir, a historical account, or an instructional book, support your work by doing the research. At the least, your readers will know if you've been lazy and at the worst, they will quickly point out when you get something wrong. If you're going to go to all the work of writing a book, take the additional steps to verify what you wrote is accurate.

The End

This is where you tie it all up, provide a solution, or demonstrate why you needed to tell your story. You'll present the take-aways you told your reader about at the beginning and you will have connected all the dots up to this point. This is the place where you summarize the reason why you told the story you've written. If you wrote an instructional book, this is where you tell the reader how much confidence you have in them for taking the steps toward enacting the solution you presented. If you've written a memoir, the reader should clearly see the change in the memoir subject by the end. Underscore what the reader has at the end of the book that they didn't have before.

Perspiration

Some would say this is where the real work starts. We like to think of it as the place where the magic happens. And if magic is work, then most writers are sorcerers and workaholics!

It can be intimidating looking at that first blank page. Fifty-thousand words seems like a lot of words when you don't even have the first word written, right?

We know what you're thinking. Where do you start?

You'd think the answer is at the beginning, right? Not necessarily. Start with what's on your mind and build around that. Some writers write linearly, from start to finish. Some writers bounce around from place to place, constructing a work as the ideas come to them, even if they have to go backward or jump ahead. Some writers do a mix of both. The trick is just to write. You can always do rewrites later—and believe us, you *will* do rewrites. (In case you forget that, we'll remind you a few more times.)

So, you've taken on this huge thing, and we bet it seems like it's getting bigger the further you read. Don't worry. It's always been the same amount of work. And remember, we're doing a lot of the heavy lifting for you by bringing all the educational material you need together, not to mention helping you to set up a successful schedule. You're going to do just fine.

But when you're getting ready to start a big project, it can seem a little overwhelming.

There's an old saying: How do you eat an elephant? One bite at a time.

Writing a book starts with a first word, which becomes a sentence, which becomes a paragraph, and the paragraphs become pages, and pages become chapters, and finally, the chapters become a book.

Writing really starts when you put your butt in your seat and open yourself up to the possibility. That's when the magic comes.

No matter how brilliant a writer is, they all start each book the same way. With a blank page and an idea. That's all you need to begin. The rest is perseverance. But trust us, once the words start flowing, momentum gets easier—until it doesn't, and we've written a chapter a little later in this section about this. It's called *Motivation, or How to keep going when the going gets tough.*

Don't worry. For now, though, just start writing. You can

always—and most definitely will—rewrite the opening lines later. In the meantime, just get started.

We'll even give you some ideas for first words:

Once upon a time...

It all started with...

They call me Ishmael...

Writing Starts with an Ugly First Draft

All books are a work in progress until they're complete.

That might sound super obvious, but understanding when a book is complete is a writer's common dilemma. They tinker and revise, and they revise and tinker. This is because it always seems like there's something to fix. A word could be different, a sentence could be structured differently, a description could be more exact. There is always a way something can be changed.

That's why writers need to understand the importance of ugly first drafts.

The overall process of writing can be unique to each writer. However, the act of writing is the same for everyone. You just need to record your words. It can be as simple as putting pencil or pen to paper, or it can be typing into a computer, recording your spoken word, or tracing words into sand.

However, most writers tend to get caught up in trying to be perfect from the first word they write. They'll spend an inordinate amount of time rewriting what they've already written, taking too much time to get to the next chapter, because the one before needs a little tinkering. Writers are weird like that. It's because words are cool and powerful, and writers are always looking for the perfect word. We're logophiles, which means lovers of words. But you already knew that.

Word to the wise—don't let your inner logophile get in your way when you're writing your first draft. Don't tinker, just write until you finish your first draft. You'll have time for rewrites later.

It may seem overly rhetorical to say that to be a writer, one must simply write. Yet this can often become the place where the want-to-be writer gets hung up, wastes a bunch of time, and just stops. Earlier in this guide, we said that the most important element of a story is the conflict. This is true. But the most important thing about writing is to write. If you don't write it, there will never be a story. A story without a conflict can be fixed. A story never written can never be fixed. (We'll probably repeat this point a few more times, too.)

What we want to do here is focus on the transition from want-to-be writer to actual writer.

The first step is to place your butt in a chair or another comfortable spot that will be conducive to writing. The right spot is a personal choice. It can be a quiet spot in your home or a meditative spot in nature. It can also be in the middle of a busy town square or at a corner table in a boisterous coffee shop. The location doesn't really matter; it's the selection of a place that makes it easiest to write for you that's important. It can also change from day to day. Maybe a certain scene is easier to write when there are absolutely no distractions. Another scene may require inspiration generated by the activity around you.

If you already know where you like to write, you are in a good spot to start. Now, you need to pick a time for when you will write. This is also different from writer to writer, and many things can influence this aspect of getting started and sticking to it. Most writers have other things going in their lives that compete for the time they have available to actually write. They have day jobs, family obligations, hobbies, homes to maintain, and an infinite variety of things that life tends to introduce just when you need fewer obligations so you can find time to write.

Our advice here is to decide where writing falls on your list of current priorities, then set aside the appropriate amount of time you can dedicate to it, and schedule it in just as you do for any other priority in your life. Sadly, some people's lives are too busy, and they have priorities that supersede a desire to write. This doesn't mean it's not possible to be a writer; it just means that those writers have to work harder to carve out the time to write.

Once you've made writing a priority in your life, it's to time to create a writing habit. It's too easy to let everyday distractions keep you from writing. That's why you need a plan. A plan will help keep you focused and prevent you from putting off something you want to do but haven't made space in your life to get done. That's where creating a habit comes in. It's well known that once a thing has become a habit, it has a greater chance of being accomplished. This goes for many things that you don't do naturally, have some reservations about, or are just trying to figure out.

So, how can you create a writing habit?

It requires making a plan, and it takes following the plan a few times to make it a habit.

How to Create a Writing Habit

- **Figure out your writing space** – This should be a place of comfort and unwanted distractions.
- **Create a writing schedule** – Find out *when* you can write and put it in your calendar.
- **Get rid of unwanted distractions** – Some people's distractions are other people's motivation. You may like the television on or listening to music when you write. You may want silence. The kinds of distractions you want to get rid of are ones that keep you from writing, which includes purging any excuses not to write.

- **Plan what you're going to write** – Some writers use an outline to guide them. Others prefer to let the words come as they will. Some start at the beginning and write all the way through, while others jump around in the story. Regardless of your process, you should have a goal that builds on the story for each writing session, even if it's merely a goal to create a new chapter about a certain plot point.

- **Keep your writing tools organized** – These are your writing implements, as well as documents like outlines, character sketches, research notes, etc. Don't waste your writing time looking for what you need. Have it handy and easy to find. For some of us, this easier to say than do.

- **Set a word count goal** – A word count is a great goal to work toward, as well as a way to estimate how long it will take you to complete your writing project. Seeing progress is a great motivator for most people. However, some writers think a word count goal is a de-motivator. Some days, words come more easily than others, and trying to meet a number when you are having trouble finding words can cause anxiety and self-doubt. If a word count stresses you out, simply set a session timer, where you focus on writing for an amount of time, rather than a number of words.

- **Write** – Write the words down. Repeat after us: *Revisions come later*. Don't reread your words (at least not to judge them—reorienting yourself in the story is okay), don't second guess them, don't over-think them, don't worry about them. Just keep writing forward. Add to the story in every session and accept that the words may not be the best words, the structure may not be perfect, and the storyline might be choppy. You will fix all of that later during revisions and edits.

- **Celebrate that you did the writing** – Brag to your friends, reward yourself with a tasty treat, take a nap, or just put a big star next to the writing session reminder in your calendar. Do something to acknowledge your hard work. You deserve it!

- **Set up your next writing session** – Do this before you leave your seat. If you don't reserve the time, it will be too easy to let the next session slide.

And, as you develop a habit, just write. Write until you have that ugly first draft. Then you can go back and tinker with it until it becomes something you'll be proud to show off.

Progress

Writing a book takes a lot of time and effort, and it's not always easy. Things invariably come up that make it difficult for us to find the energy or motivation to continue. Sometimes, just knowing that a book will eventually be completed isn't enough to keep a writer going—especially when doubts or other obstacles pop up along the way.

One of the best motivators to keep going on a long project is simply knowing that you're making steady progress toward a specific goal. The goal can be the end result of having a finished manuscript or a published book in your hands. Or it can be a daily goal of having spent time writing, getting a chapter written, or meeting a certain daily word count.

The *Inkslinger – 99-Day Guided Writing Experience* helps you monitor your progress by setting an end goal and daily writing goals that will help you successfully get through completing your Inkslinger manuscript. In order to do this, we have set a designated writing goal of 50,000 words to be written over the 80-day writing portion of your 99-day project. The first five days consist of planning your story, and the last fourteen days are used for revisions and self-edits. The 80-day middle portion is when you sit down and write regularly to meet the goal of writing your story in 50,000 words.

You may be wondering if you can write more than 50,000 words during the **Inkslinger – 99-Day Guided Writing Experience**. Sure! How about fewer? Yes, to that, too. If you have a different word count in mind, feel free to adjust your schedule to reflect the words you need to write over the 80-day writing portion of the schedule. The 50,000 goal is there to help you, not constrain you.

But how did we come up with 50,000 words for your first draft manuscript then? Simple! It's a good round number that isn't too overwhelming when broken into 80-days of writing sprints. It's a little longer than a typical novella, which is usually between 30,000 to 40,000 words long, and it's on the short end of the novel-length story, which begins at around 50,000 words and goes longer—sometimes much, much longer!

The Inkslinger 50,000-word count is an easily accomplished goal when you plan it correctly and sit down and do the work—and we give you all the tools you need to do that.

In a future section, we will give you a way to determine how many words you must write each day to reach the 50,000-word count goal. We've provided several options to choose from based on the number of days you commit to writing during this project. There is nothing preventing you from taking more or less time, or writing more or fewer words for your project, but it may be difficult to successfully complete your project if you don't adhere to the goals we've prescribed. But, hey! If you feel up to it, go for it. Each writer is different.

Research

Research comes with the territory when you're a writer. The amount of research needed for any given book is determined by the subject matter of the story and the amount of knowledge the writer brings to the project. Some writers dive deep into research, while others do as little as possible. There is no rule about how much research a writer needs to do. The important thing is that the story must be accurate, otherwise your readers will tell you if it's not, and you don't want that. One of the most embarrassing things that can happen to a writer is to get all the way through completing and publishing their story, just to have a reader point out that they got something wrong. Correcting a published novel requires a lot of work—more than you might expect.

So, heed our advice—do your research.

Aren't there people for that, you ask. Sure. If you're Stephen King, or one of the wildly successful writers who have a staff working for them. Until then, it's all up to you to do the work.

What about editors, you counter.

Editors will help find and correct typos and grammatical errors, and there are content editors who may find some informational errors, but it's not feasible to expect any editor to double check every fact in a manuscript. It's on the writer to ensure that they depict all information provided in their story as accurately as possible.

Some writers may look at writing as a purely creative endeavor. The world they build is unique to the book, and all elements are a result of the creative process. And this is true to a certain extent. Many genres include creative world-building and the invention of things that have not been seen in our world. But even those kinds of books require the writer to keep track of what they have already written to prevent the reader from being pulled out of the story because something sounds off. Don't expect your readers not to notice the smallest incorrect detail. They will. And they will tell people.

So, whether your story requires considerable research or minimal research, make sure you take the time to verify the information you put into your story, and that you pay attention to consistency within your own story.

Some advice on *when* to perform research; it is extremely easy to fall into a Google search rabbit hole if you're not careful, and this can eat up valuable writing time. One way you can avoid this is by setting aside dedicated research time. Also, you should collect your research topics so you can do several of them at once, which will save you some time and possibly keep you focused. A trick to doing this is to make research a preliminary step before starting the writing of your story. Look up the information you think you'll need and take notes or collect data to reference when you're writing. If you find you need to do some research while you're writing, make a note in your manuscript where you need to look something up and go back to it later. You can do this in line and highlight it so you can find it later, or you can make a note by embedding a comment if you're using a word-processing program.

The Hook

The first line is ideally the hook, but it's not always the first line. It can be the first few paragraphs or pages. Either way, hooks are an important way to grab the reader's attention in your story and keep them interested.

That's what it's all about, right? Getting people to like your story.

Many readers read the first lines of a book they pick up to decide if the story is intriguing enough to buy and spend their time reading. They are also figuring out whether the writing is up to their standards and getting an idea about what to expect from the story. In essence, they're building a first opinion.

And we all know first opinions are important. You only get one chance, and happy readers are the best way to market your books—this one and the ones after it. If they give up on you once, they probably won't come back.

Don't give a reader a reason *not* to read your story by starting off with an uninteresting first line.

Check out these unforgettable first lines by authors:

> "It is a truth universally acknowledged, that a single man in possession of a good fortune must be in want of a wife."
>
> > – *Pride and Prejudice,* **Jane Austin**

> "Far out in the uncharted backwaters of the unfashionable end of the Western Spiral arm of the Galaxy lies a small unregarded yellow sun. Orbiting this at a distance of roughly ninety-eight million miles is an utterly insignificant little blue-green planet whose ape-descended life forms are so amazingly primitive that they still think digital watches are a pretty neat idea."
>
> > – *Hitchhiker's Guide to the Galaxy,*
> > **Douglas Adams**

> "You better not never tell nobody but God."
>
> > — *The Color Purple,* **Alice Walker**

> "It was a queer, sultry summer, the summer they electrocuted the Rosenbergs, and I didn't know what I was doing in New York."
>
> > – *The Bell Jar,* **Sylvia Plath**

> "We were somewhere around Barstow, on the edge of the desert, when the drugs began to take hold"
>
> > – *Fear and Loathing in Las Vegas,*
> > **Hunter S Thompson**

"Can you imagine valuing a book so much that you send the author a Thank You letter?"

– Project Management Professional (PMP) Exam Prep Seventh Edition: Rita's Course in a Book for Passing the PMP Exam, **Rita Mulcahy**

Here's a list of ideas about how to write an effective hook:

- Engage the reader's curiosity
- Start it off with a compelling narrative voice
- Illicit strong emotion
- Surprise your reader
- Make it strange or captivating
- Tease with information
- Introduce the conflict immediately
- Make the reader think
- Introduce an interesting character

Show, Don't Tell

If there is a Golden Rule in writing, it is **Show, Don't Tell**.

Showing, not telling, is the difference between a boring story and a compelling story. It's the difference between experiencing the story and following along with the story. It's the difference between a good book and an "eh" book. It's the difference between a reader checking out the sample of your book and not buying it and a reader becoming a fan who buys all your books.

Show, don't tell is when a writer presents the story through actions and sensory details, rather than explaining what's going on through exposition. This allows the reader to experience the story. Showing provides richer detail, often inferring more than is stated, giving the reader an opportunity to add to the scene through their own experience and imagination.

Anton Chekhov may have said it best when he said: *"Don't*

tell me the moon is rising, show me the glint of light on broken glass."

Pretty powerful, huh?

Which do you like better?

> **Telling:** *Becky was frustrated when her mother told her she couldn't go to the dance.*
>
> **Showing:** *After spending an entire day picking out a new dress, and after weeks of devising clever ways to ask Billy to dance with her, Becky banged her head against the paneled wall of her father's study. "But, Daddy, why? Why must mother make me babysit my stupid brother tonight, of all nights?"*

Most stories will contain some elements of telling. Exposition has value. It's often less wordy and can be useful in quickly transitioning scenes. In fact, many great stories begin with telling through exposition to set the scene, and readers can get a little fatigued when there's nothing but dialogue and action. So, there is a place and time for telling. But showing when you can show should be a primary goal for a writer and will enhance the experience for the reader.

Transformation

One of the sweetest moments for any writer is writing the words "The End."

You've written tens of thousands of words. You've produced a manuscript with a beginning, a middle, and an end. You've brought a world to life with your words. Most importantly, you've given birth to a story that has been rattling around in your mind for weeks, months, or even years.

You should take a little time to acknowledge your achievement. Not everyone can say they've written a complete manuscript. You're among a small, elite group of people.

It's a good feeling and one you should hold onto and enjoy.

It's time to celebrate! Really celebrate. Treat yourself to a nice dinner. Buy yourself a gift. Crack open that bottle of scotch you've been saving for a special day. Reward yourself your own way. You. Earned. It.

The next phase is the transformation of your ugly first draft into a revised manuscript that will be ready to send to an editor.

During this phase, you will read through your first draft, maybe make updates to the story, look for typos, smooth out clunky sentences, deal with some troublesome words, and basically spiff up your manuscript.

Rewrites, Revisions, Self-edits, Oh My!

Transformation of an ugly first draft into a real manuscript is as much of the creative process as the actual writing, and rewrites are the way you will transform your caterpillar of a story into a butterfly of a story.

Rewrites aka revisions aka self-edits are what make good writing great. You get to improve on what you've already written by making the piece tighter and more to the point, tweaking your work to make it perfect. This is where you get to spend time looking for the perfect word or phrase to make your story pop.

Rewrites are a necessary part of a writer's process. Some writers love them. (We do!) And some writers love them *not*. In fact, when writers *don't* love rewrites, they tend to come up with some pretty descriptive words to convey their feelings—words such as despise, abhor, hate, dread, diabolical, tedious, and annoying come to mind. In an unscientific survey of our writer friends, it seems the loves and loves nots are about evenly split.

We get it. You've just written your masterpiece. You really want it to be done. But you're not done yet. You still need to put on the finishing touches to make sure you're presenting the best piece of writing you are capable of. It's tedious. We know. But do it. You'll be happy you did, and your future editor will be even happier.

So, what do rewrites entail?

The following are the steps you'll take to transform your story into a work you will be proud to send off to a professional editor. We've broken it down into a process that starts with the broad strokes and finishes with the finer details.

Read your manuscript aloud

To get started, read your manuscript out loud at least once through. Not only is it a nice way to revel in your accomplishment, you'll be able to determine clunky phrasing and sentence structure when you find yourself struggling to read through certain areas. If you have a problem reading through it, you can bet your readers will, too.

As you read, take notes, but don't correct any major issues immediately. You want to wait until you've finished the read-through to identify any other possible issues you'll want to address. Also, believe it or not, you'll have forgotten some of what you've written, and there is a chance the issue might be resolved in the next pages, but you just don't remember it. Trust us, this is more common than you think. Feel free to correct minor things, such as typos, grammar issues, and specific word changes if you like, though. Just save the major changes until you've identified them all.

Start with the big picture

The first thing you want to do when looking for revisions is to start generally. Taking a look at the story with the big picture in mind will help you spot issues such as plot holes, unresolved plot points, mistakes in timelines, inconsistencies in the story, and other issues. You'll examine what you're trying to get across and revise any big swaths of mushy writing to make them tighter. By "mushy" we mean writing that can be written more concisely and clearly, or maybe cut out altogether. An example of what can be cut might be repeated information in an attempt to make sure the reader understood what you were trying to convey. That's a perfect opportunity to combine multiple iterations of the same information into a single instance with more clarity. Or you may find that you've become too wordy or even added something that doesn't move the story forward. Even if the writing is brilliant, if it doesn't move the story forward, it doesn't belong.

Ensure each paragraph is interesting and transitions smoothly

Next, go through each paragraph to make sure the writing is interesting. If a paragraph isn't interesting, it either needs to be cut or revised. Each paragraph should open with an interesting sentence and end with a sentence that transitions smoothly to the next paragraph. If the paragraphs don't smoothly transition, the story will feel disjointed and the reader may get confused about what they're reading.

Seek and destroy filter words, pet words, and too frequently used words

Something to look for while you're reviewing your manuscript are pet words. These are words that a writer might use while speaking but don't translate very well to the written page. Often, these are filler words. While they might work well in some dialogue, they don't belong in the narrative—unless you're trying to give your narrator a specific voice, and when used in that way, they should be used sparingly. Some examples of pet words are; okay, so, then, hey, oh, etc.

Another example is filter words, which are sense verbs that create a distance between the reader and the story, reminding us that we're reading, rather than experiencing the story. Remember: **Show, Don't Tell**. Examples are: see, saw, noticed, realized, thought, seemed, and others.

This is telling:

I heard the birds singing.

This is showing:

The chorus of bird song reminded us that spring had finally arrived.

A big difference, right?

Finally, keep a lookout for unique words that can stand out to a reader. Words like gobsmacked, bucolic, ubiquitous, apropos, and fortuitous can be wonderfully used but will probably push the reader out of the story if seen more than once. Of course, this is very dependent on context, type of story being told, the writer's particular voice, the chosen POV, as well as the expected target audience.

Mix up sentence structure

Repetition can be a major turn off to a reader, and this doesn't only apply to the use of words. Sentence structure can become repetitive, too. And it can go either way—too many complex sentences in a row can make a reader work too hard, and too many short sentences can bore them. Be aware of the cadence of your writing to make sure your reader is provided an interesting mix of short and complex sentences.

Keep listening for your story's voice

Think about your favorite book. Did that book have a unique voice that remained consistent throughout the story? Do you "hear" the narrator's voice when just remembering this book? That's probably the reason why you call it your favorite book. The voice of a book is largely the result of the writer's style. It's a combination of many things: the words, phrases, execution, tone, and many other things that serve to give the story a distinct personality. Some writers have a voice so powerful or unique you can sense it in every story they write. Others like to change their voice from story to story. When going through rewrites, make sure the voice of the story remains consistent.

And finally:

The odds and ends

As you're doing revisions, look for:

- Typos
- Proper capitalization
- Tense changes
- The use of passive voice – Passive voice is a stylistic choice that can make a scene feel sluggish and wordy. Active voice is the preferred style for most writing. Passive voice is when a writer makes the object of an action into the subject of a sentence.

Example:

> **Passive Voice**: *The child was bitten by the dog.*
>
> **Active Voice**: *The dog bit the child.*

- POV consistency
- Too many adverbs – these are usually words that end in -ly, but not always. While it is not terrible to use adverbs, they tend to be over-used and clutter sentences, and they tend to be linked to less showing and more telling.
- Too many sentences starting with "she" or "he"
- Too much usage of complex sentences in a group (fatigues the reader)
- Too much usage of short or simple sentences in a group (bores the reader)
- Too much usage of anything
- "Pet" words or words you overuse – We suggest that you keep a list of pet words to look for as you discover them in your writing.

A word of caution on doing rewrites: the goal is to produce the best written work you are capable of. However, some writers will rewrite forever if you let them. There is always something that can be changed. But you need to stop at some point. When you find yourself making tiny tweaks that make very little difference, stop. You're done.

Motivation

Keeping motivated, or as many writers like to refer to it, **how to keep going when the going gets tough**, is a real thing. It happens to every writer: a day comes when they find it hard to keep writing. It's not that they don't want to write. Well, sometimes it is. All of us have those days when we'd rather be doing something other than what we planned to do. But it's usually something else that comes up, thwarting us from writing. It could be an internal issue, or it might be something outside our control. It's easy when it's outside of our control. We can do things like write the thing into our story and kill them off. That'll show them! It's the internal issues that are usually the hardest to deal with.

What if my story sucks?

What if I don't know the things I need to know about writing?

What if I get writer's block?

What if I don't have 50,000 words to share?

What if I get behind?

How do I stay motivated if I get bored with the story?

It's inevitable. There *will* come times during the process when it's hard to keep going. Insecurities creep in. Ideas hang just out of reach. Distractions steal our focus and our time. Heck, even boredom creeps in when we're expanding on the backstory or trying to add depth to our plotline. (It's called the "mushy middle" for a reason!) It can't all be chase scenes and big reveals. Sometimes our characters define themselves through being normal everyday people. Where's the magic in *that*?

The answer is that magic can happen anywhere. It's when you weave the perfect combination of emotion into a scene. It can be that perfect word that completes the perfect sentence. It can be the unique way a plotline evolves. Or it can simply be a single phrase that becomes the heart of the entire story. There are infinite possibilities to create the magic, and honestly, it usually comes when you aren't even expecting it.

But when the going gets tough, it's hard to keep moving toward the goal.

Here are some ideas to stay motivated.

- Make writing a habit. This is the single most effective way to keep going.
- Set goals – daily, weekly, monthly – whatever it takes.
- Don't expect brilliance. Not all words are going to

shine the first time, but if you have words, write them down. You can always rewrite the scene when the brilliant words are erupting from your fertile mind.

- When you're feeling insecure, write about it. Not in the story—separately. Journaling can often allow your mind to let go of worries, even if you don't have solutions.
- Don't edit as you write. It will bog you down. Edits can come at the end, after you've written your first draft.
- Get as much of the idea as you have down and come back to it.
- Put your plot points onto pieces of paper, put them in a hat, and pick one out. Write that scene instead of writing from start to end.
- Write in fragmented sentences to just get something written, knowing you can expand on it later.
- When you get stuck on a specific scene or chapter, make a note that you need to get back to it and then move to the next scene.
- Don't force it. It may not be the right time or the right scene.
- Get a writing buddy, someone you feel accountable to for getting your work done.
- Make writing dates with your writing buddy and write together.
- Some people enjoy music when they write.
- Talk to someone about your story.
- Join a writing group.

- Read a book.
- Switch up your writing area.
- Try writing with pen and paper if you usually write on a computer, or vice versa.
- Remind yourself why you want to be a writer.
- Take a break.
- Take a nap.

And finally, celebrate the small stuff. It's important. Writing isn't always fun, and when it isn't, a little celebration may be what you need to keep you going by giving yourself something to look forward to.

Earlier in this book, in the *Writing Starts with an Ugly First Draft* chapter, we mentioned that you should create a writing habit. And as part of that habit, we suggested that you should celebrate that you did the writing.

We can't oversell the power of positive reinforcement when it comes to writing.

Once you finish your first book, you will have fulfilled a dream, and there is nothing quite comparable to holding a finished manuscript or book in your hands. Even successful writers who have completed a number of books get a tingle in their belly when they write the wonderful words "The End" or when they get to open the box on book delivery day. However, it takes a lot of work and overcoming of insecurities and lack of knowledge to get to the point where you're holding that manuscript or book in your hand. We're not going to lie: some days will be worse than others.

So, one of the things you can do for yourself is to celebrate the little things along the way. Celebrations can be big or small, but make them meaningful enough that they keep you wanting to move forward. You can do this by giving yourself a treat when you successfully meet or exceed a word count goal. Or you can give yourself a shout out on social media, telling your friends that you finished a tough chapter. If you have a good day and get double your word count, take a day off—or better yet, stay ahead in your word count goals to relieve the pressure for when you have a less than stellar word count day later on. Whatever it is, make it something you look forward to or can look back on, feeling good about all your hard work.

This is where the fun begins!

Part II is where we help you create a schedule broken into three parts that will result in you writing a 50,000-word revised manuscript that will be ready to give to a professional editor.

Inspiration – Plan your story

Perspiration – Write your story

Transformation – Revise your story

Welcome to the fun, Writer! This is where it really starts!

Welcome to your *Inkslinger – 99-Day Guided Writing Experience*!

If you follow the guide on the next several pages, you will successfully complete a book.

Will it be good? Of course, it will!

Will it be awesome? Hell, yes!

Will it be hard? Most definitely?

Will it be worth it? 100%!

Will people read it? That depends on you. Writing the book is definitely the hardest part. But there are lots of things that still need to be done. You can choose to do all of them or none of them, but the important thing is: at the end of 99 days you will have written a book. You can be proud of that.

Having read each of the previous sections of this guide, you are ready to start the 99-day timer.

This is exciting! You're starting a book, and in 99 days you will have completed a manuscript that you can transform into a real-life, honest to goodness, hold in your hands BOOK!

If you have never considered yourself a writer before, this is when you get to do it. Say it out loud.

I am a writer.

Now scream it. Go ahead and scare your neighbors, or the guy sitting next to you at the coffee shop.

I am a writer!

Do you have chills? We do!

Your Inkslinger – 99-Day Guided Writing Experience

This is what you've been working toward by reading all the previous pages, getting prepared to write your story.

We're done with our words. It's time for yours.

Your schedule starts on the next page.

Days One through Five – Inspiration

Worksheets

You have eight worksheets to complete in the first five days.

Day 1

Worksheet 1 – Target Audience

Worksheet 2 – Genre

Day 2

Worksheet 3 – Story Arc and Plot

Day 3

Worksheet 4 – Outline

Day 4

Worksheet 5 – Point of View (POV)

Worksheet 6 – Setting

Day 5

Worksheet 7 – Character Sketches

Worksheet 8 – Conflict

We went over the topics of each of these worksheets in the Part I of this guide, so you can reference the related sections to help you fill out your worksheets.

Sample worksheets are provided on the next pages along with a schedule of which worksheets to do on each day. Three of the days you will have two worksheets to complete and two days you only have one worksheet to complete, but the one worksheet days are a little more complex than the two worksheet days. However, you can do all the worksheets on one day if you're feeling ambitious.

You can download digital version of the worksheets at:

https://inkstacks.com/inkslinger/download-worksheets/

You can access the worksheets for free to either save to your own computer and fill out online, or print them out to fill them out by hand.

Day One

Worksheet 1 – Target Audience Worksheet

inkslinger
99-Day Guided Writing Experience

Target Audience Worksheet

- What kind of story, or genre, are you writing? (Genres often come with a specific audience already identified)
- Why are you writing this particular story?
- What message do you want your story to impart?
- Is there a specific audience who the message will best suit?

Demographics

Category	Target Audience
Age	
Location	
Gender	
Income	
Education	
Marital or Family Status	
Occupation	
Ethnic Background	

Notes

inkstacks.com/inkslinger/target-audience

Worksheet 2 – Genre Worksheet

inkslinger
99-Day Guided Writing Experience

Genre Worksheet

Sometimes writers know exactly what kind of books or stories they want to write. Other times, they have a hard time pinning their preferred genre down. And sometimes, a story can contain elements of multiple genres. An example of this might be a story about the civil war that also contains romance. Or a story about young people fighting against a corrupt government in the future. The genre of your book will fall within the category that is most prominent in the story. If it feels like there is an even amount of time dedicated to one element or another, you get to pick which one you like, and the others can be assigned as sub-genres.

To see a list of writing genres visit: https://en.wikipedia.org/wiki/List_of_writing_genres

What kind of books do you like to read?	Refer to the genre guide (see link above) and find the genre that best fits your answer:
Are there things you don't want to read or write about?	Refer to the genre guide (see link above) and find the genre that best fits your answer:
Are there certain tropes (cliches) you're drawn to or don't care for?	Refer to the genre guide (see link above) and find the genre that best fits your answer:
Is there a specific message you want to get across?	Refer to the genre guide (see link above) and find the genre that best fits your answer:
What audience do I want to reach?	Refer to the genre guide (see link above) and find the genre that best fits your answer:
Are there certain settings you like to write about?	Refer to the genre guide (see link above) and find the genre that best fits your answer:
What conflicts in stories do you like to write about?	Refer to the genre guide (see link above) and find the genre that best fits your answer:
What other details about genre do you find appealing?	Refer to the genre guide (see link above) and find the genre that best fits your answer:

What genre(s) appears most frequently here?

Despite the findings on this form, is there a genre that stands out to you? That is likely the genre you should write in.

inkstacks.com/inkslinger/genre

Day Two

Worksheet 3 – Story Arc and Plot Worksheet

Story Arc Worksheet

inkslinger
99-Day Guided Writing Experience

Theme:

Climax:

The Story Arc

Exposition: Introduces the main character(s) to the reader, tells what problem is to be solved, and sets the place and tone. Main character(s) and problem to be solved, inciting incident, setting time, setting place.

Rising Action: The build up of tension to the climax explaining what the story is about and contains the inciting incident.

Climax: This is the main character(s)' moment of truth.

Falling Action: Describes the consequences to the actions of the character(s), tying up loose ends.

Resolution: How the story ends, closing the loop of the story.

Major Plot Points

9. _____

8. _____

7. _____

6. _____

5. _____

4. _____

3. _____

2. _____

1. _____

Falling Action

Rising Action

10. _____

11. _____

12. _____

13. _____

14. _____

Resolution:

Exposition:

inkstacks.com/inkslinger/story-arc

Day Three

Worksheet 4 – Outline Worksheet

inkslinger
99-Day Guided Writing Experience

Outline Worksheet

Beat Sheet

Story Title:

Story Blurb:

Beats	Detail	Chapter(s)
Act One	**Reader hook introduces characters, exposition, set up major conflict**	
Inciting Incident	What starts the characters on their journey?	
Begin the Rising Action	What events force the characters forward?	
Act Two	**What conflicts occur to force the characters forward?**	
Minor conflict #1	Increase the tension with additional conflict.	
Midpoint	Explain why the character(s) must go forward.	
Minor conflict #2	Increase the tension with additional conflict.	
Crisis	What makes the characters doubt they will succeed?	
Act Three	**The main character(s) overcomes hurdles to succeed**	
Climax	What is the turning point in the story?	
Resolution	What did the character(s) learn or how did they change?	

Notes

inkstacks.com/inkslinger/outline

Day Four

Worksheet 5 – Point of View (POV) Worksheet

inkslinger
99-Day Guided Writing Experience

Point of View (POV) Worksheet

Determining What Point of View (POV) to Use in Your Story:

Select the description that makes the most sense for your story in respect to each of the following five questions.

Use additional note pages at end for any notes you would like to take.

1. **How much distance do you want to put between the reader and the narrator?**

    A. You want the reader to feel like they are in the mind of the characters

    B. You want the reader to feel like they are literally a character in the story.

    C. You want to leave a certain amount of distance between the narrator and the reader.

2. **How much information do you need to convey to the reader throughout the story?**

    A. You want the reader to know everything happening in this story.

    B. You need to instruct the reader on how to do things.

    C. You want to keep a sense of mystery about one or more aspects of the story.

3. **How reliable do you want the narrator to be?**

    A. It is most important that the reader feel a connection to the character, even if the character is flawed.

    B. The narrator needs to talk directly to the reader.

    C. You want the reader to rely on the narrator as a trusted source of all aspects of the story.

4. **What kind and how much information do you need to provide to the reader?**

    A. One or more characters have information that needs to be conveyed to the reader without letting other characters know.

    B. The book is a step-by-step instruction on how to do something.

    C. You nee to reveal a surprise climax or ending that none of the characters see coming.

5. **How important is developing a connection between the reader and the characters?**

    A. There is a specific character you want the reader to connect with.

    B. You want the reader to be the direct focus of the narrator.

    C. You want the reader to connect to several characters.

What your selections mean: if you picked mostly:

    A. You probably want to write your story with a First Person point of view.

    B. You are probably writing a How To book and Second Person will be an effective point of view.

    C. Third Person point of view will probably be your preferred point of view.

Keep in mind, these are just suggestions. Only you know the best point of view in which to tell your story. Authors are creative and like to bend the "rules" so if that's you, do your thing and have fun!

When in doubt, Third Person point of view is effective in almost all kinds of stories.

inkstacks.com/inkslinger/point-of-view

Worksheet 6 – Setting Worksheet

inkslinger
99-Day Guided Writing Experience

Setting Worksheet

Story Title:

Story Blurb:

Where does the story take place? List the settings with a short description:

When does the story take place? List the times/ periods:

What are the moods of the settings?

Day Five

Worksheet 7 – Character Sketch Worksheet

inkslinger
99-Day Guided Writing Experience

Character Sketch Worksheet

Story Title:

Story Blurb:

Character Name:

Physical Description:

Character Traits:

What is their motivation (desires)?

What do they fear?

Where do they live?

Who are their friends, family, pets?

inkstacks.com/inkslinger/character-sketch

Worksheet 8 – Conflict Worksheet

inkslinger
99-Day Guided Writing Experience

Conflict Worksheet

Story Title:

Character:

Internal Conflict: A character has conflict within themselves.

Internal Conflict:

Actions/
reactions:

External Conflict: The conflict is outside of the character's control.

External Conflict:

Actions/
reactions:

inkstacks.com/inkslinger/conflict

Days Six through Eighty-five - Perspiration

Writing your 50,000-word manuscript.

This is the heart and soul of Inkslinger.

Now that you have all the information you need to know about writing from the previous sections, you're ready to do the actual writing.

In order to write a book, you need to write. Hopefully, you've picked up on this point because we've repeated it over and over. Maybe you're even a little tired of the repetition. But it cannot be emphasized enough that a book is only a book once it's been written.

To make it simple, we've distilled this part into the following steps:

1. Figure out a writing schedule. (See the below table

for guidance.)

2. Put reminders in your personal calendar to write your daily words (and do it!).
3. Tell someone you're doing this, or better yet, get a buddy to do it with you. (It's easier to complete something if you feel accountable to someone.)
4. Find a comfortable place without distractions.
5. Sit your butt in the chair.
6. Write.
7. Repeat every day of the schedule you've selected for the next eighty days.

It really is this simple.

Words Needed Per Day to Reach 50,000 Words in the Next 80 Days

Words needed per day to reach 50,000 words in 80 days

625	...if you write every day for the next 80 days
725	...if you write six days per week and give yourself one day off to chill
862	...if you write five days per week and take the weekends off to hang with the fam, friends
2,174	...if you write only on weekends which will be 23 days of the next 80 days
Insert Your Number Here	...if you have another schedule in mind—just figure out the number of days you have in the next 80 and divide the number of days by 50,000 to get "your number"
50,000	...if you wait until the last day to cram it all at once (NOT RECOMMENEDED unless you are a masochist or a really, really fast writer)

Before we go on to the next step, let's do a little recap:

You decided to write a book!

You spent time absorbing the basic information we've provided about writing a book.

You spent five days of your 99-day guided path planning what you're going to write.

Are you ready for the fun part?

You have 80 days to write 50,000 words.

Let's go!

Sample Calendar

Check out the following of a sample calendar for a view of what the schedule you selected might look like in your personal calendar.

In this example, the writer has chosen to write six days a week, giving themselves a day off. This gives them sixty-nine days of writing, which makes their daily word count 725 words a day. Also, note there is one day during the schedule, on March 12, where the writer needs to take an unexpected day off. They make up for the day they missed by doing double the daily wordcount the next day.

For incentive, this writer has scheduled weekly check-ins with a writing buddy. This is a great way to incorporate accountability into their project. It's always more fun when you have a friend to share your goals with!

99 days may seem like a long time, but having a visual like this really helps make a task like writing an entire book seem doable!

January

Sunday	Monday	Tuesday	Wednesday	Thursday	Friday	Saturday
					1 Worksheets 1 & 2 Check-In w/buddy	**2** Worksheet 3
3 Worksheet 4	**4** Worksheets 5 & 6	**5** Worksheet 7 & 8	**6** Write 725 Words	**7** Write 725 Words	**8** Write 725 Words Check-in w/buddy	**9** Write 725 Words
10 Day Off	**11** Write 725 Words	**12** Write 725 Words	**13** Write 725 Words	**14** Write 725 Words	**15** Write 725 Words Check-in w/buddy	**16** Write 725 Words
17 Day Off	**18** Write 725 Words	**19** Write 725 Words	**20** Write 725 Words	**21** Write 725 Words	**22** Write 725 Words Check-in w/buddy	**23** Write 725 Words
24 Day Off	**25** Write 725 Words	**26** Write 725 Words	**27** Write 725 Words	**28** Write 725 Words	**29** Write 725 Words Check-in w/buddy	**30** Write 725 Words 15,950 words
31 Day Off						

February

Sunday	Monday	Tuesday	Wednesday	Thursday	Friday	Saturday
	1 Write 725 Words	**2** Write 725 Words	**3** Write 725 Words	**4** Write 725 Words	**5** Write 725 Words Check-In w/buddy	**6** Write 725 Words
7 Day Off	**8** Write 725 Words	**9** Write 725 Words	**10** Write 725 Words	**11** Write 725 Words	**12** Write 725 Words Check-in w/buddy	**13** Write 725 Words
14 Day Off	Halfway! **15** Write 725 Words 25,375 words	**16** Write 725 Words	**17** Write 725 Words	**18** Write 725 Words	**19** Write 725 Words Check-in w/buddy	**20** Write 725 Words
21 Day Off	**22** Write 725 Words	**23** Write 725 Words	**24** Write 725 Words	**24** Write 725 Words	**26** Write 725 Words Check-in w/buddy	**27** Write 725 Words 33,350 words
28 Day Off						

March

Sunday	Monday	Tuesday	Wednesday	Thursday	Friday	Saturday
	1 Write 725 Words	**2** Write 725 Words	**3** Write 725 Words	**4** Write 725 Words	**5** Write 725 Words Check-in w/buddy	**6** Write 725 Words
7 Day Off	**8** Write 725 Words	**9** Write 725 Words	**10** Write 725 Words	**11** Write Unexpected Day Off	**12** Write 1450 Words Check-in w/buddy	**13** Write 725 Words
14 Day Off	**15** Write 725 Words	**16** Write 725 Words	**17** Write 725 Words	**18** Write 725 Words	**19** Write 725 Words Check-in w/buddy	**20** Write 725 Words
21 Day Off	**22** Write 725 Words	**23** Write 725 Words	**24** Write 725 Words	**24** Write 725 Words	**26** Write 700 Words Congratulations!	**27** Self Edits Check-in w/buddy
28 Self Edits	**29** Self Edits	**30** Self Edits	**31** Self Edits			

April

Sunday	Monday	Tuesday	Wednesday	Thursday	Friday	Saturday
				1 Self Edits	**2** Self Edits	**3** Self Edits Check-in w/buddy
4 Self Edits	**5** Self Edits	**6** Self Edits Check-in w/buddy	**7** Self Edits	**8** Day 99 Self Edits	**9** Self Edits	**10** Celebrate!

Day Eighty-six—Celebration

Write your final day word count including the glorious words:

> # "The End"

Take a deep breath and let it out. You did it.

We wrote this Haiku for you:

> *No words are sweeter*
>
> *To a writer than "The End"*
>
> *We celebrate now!*

Give yourself a present for getting to this point.

Days Eighty-seven through Ninety-nine—Transformation

Rewrites. See the chapter titled Transformation in Part I for the details we provided for rewrites.

1. Read your entire story out loud, taking notes on things you want to change.
2. Start with the big picture.
3. Ensure each paragraph is interesting and transitions smoothly.
4. Seek and destroy pet words and too frequently used words.
5. Mix up sentence structure.
6. Keep listening for your story's voice.
7. Address the odds and ends.
   - Typos
   - Proper capitalization
   - Tense changes

- The use of passive voice
- POV consistency
- Too many adverbs
- Too many sentences starting with "she" or "he"
- Too much usage of complex sentences in a group (fatigues the reader)
- Too much usage of short or simple sentences in a group (bores the reader)
- Too much usage of anything
- "Pet" words or words you overuse. We suggest that you keep a list of pet words to look for as you discover them in your writing.

What Comes Next?

Congratulations! You have completed the *Inkslinger – 99-Day Guided Writing Experience*!

Now that you have a revised manuscript in your hands, there is a world of possibility!

Some writers write for themselves. Other writers are content to have a story to share with a small group of family or friends. Many writers have dreams of becoming published authors. The question is: what do you want to do with your manuscript?

If what you wanted to do was write a well-written story for yourself or to share with your family and friends, well, congratulations! You've done it! You can even have your manuscript bound into an honest-to-goodness book by any number of printing companies for a fee. Your book can be a lovely and thoughtful gift you and your family and friends will cherish.

For those writers who dream of publication, there are a number of paths for you to consider. Each one of these paths is worthy of its own guide, and because this guide is intended to get a writer to this point in the process, we'll provide just a quick overview of the most common publication paths and a quick synopsis so you can get an idea of where to go from here on your own.

Deciding Not to Publish

Some stories are meant to remain a personal accomplishment, and that's just fine. There are countless reasons people might not want to go through a formal publishing process, but privacy, expense, and additional effort are probably the top reasons. We have grandparents who have put all the effort into writing the family history just to share with others. This kind of story might not be worth the extra time and expense of formally publishing it, but it doesn't take away any of the triumph of having written a fully revised manuscript. Family members will still be able to pass it on to one another and enjoy it for generations to come.

Self-publishing

Self-publishing has become a common path for writers in the last decade, thanks to the expansion of digital technology. This publishing path provides authors with the most flexibility and creativity in getting their books published. It also cuts out most of the go-betweens, so authors maintain most of the profits. For the same reason, getting the book distributed can be fast and easy.

Quality is probably the one aspect of self-publishing that gets the most scrutiny. The reason for this is primarily because many authors don't want to invest much money into the production of their books. The number one criticism is that many authors fail to ensure that their book is thoroughly and professionally edited. This has led to a certain segment of readers who will not buy self-published books because they don't trust the quality.

If an author is fairly knowledgeable and is willing to put the time and money into it, this publishing path can be the most lucrative option. It also allows the author the most control because they make all the decisions.

There have been numerous success stories about authors who self-published and became best sellers. They are few and far between, but it is possible.

Traditional Publishing

Traditional publishing is what most people think of when publishing a book. This is the world in which writers have agents who pitch their books to the big publishing houses, sign contracts, and get paid advances. Most well-known authors are associated with the "Big Five" publishing firms.

If you truly want a publisher to hold your hand and make the publishing process as easy as possible, trying to sign on with a traditional publisher is the way to go. It isn't simple to get picked up by a traditional publisher, though. It takes time, a lot of pitching, and having the book the publisher is looking for. And once you've signed a contract with a traditional firm, you are locked in until the contract you sign says otherwise.

This publishing path has some really great aspects, but it comes with a good share of what to some may not be so great aspects, as well.

Some of the advantages of having a traditional publisher are:

- Not having to know as much about the ins and outs of the technical aspects or the business side of the industry
- Not having to pay for all the details required to manage the production and administration of the book
- They usually pay advances
- Access to expert guidance in all aspects of the publishing process
- Established markets, which usually leads to higher sales
- High quality production standards
- Inherent credibility of being associated with a known company brand

Some of the challenges associated with going with a traditional publisher are:

- Almost always need to have an agent, which cuts into royalties
- Contracted royalty percentages are often lower than self-published, boutique, or hybrid publishers
- Writers have limited creative liberty
- The publishing company owns the creative rights
- More authors competing for individualized support from the company
- Higher pressure to sell books in order to get future book contracts

Our advice for authors who want to sign up with a traditional publishing company: read the contract carefully.

Boutique Publishing or Hybrid Publishing

Boutique, or Hybrid publishers, are usually small publishing companies who specialize in focused areas of publication. They may feature specific genres that have a limited market, or they may provide specialized services for their writers. This concentration on specific aspects in publishing can be beneficial to writers who are looking for expertise in their area of writing, as the boutique publishers often have niche knowledge to apply that may not be available with a traditional publishing company. Also, this specialization often limits the number of writers being managed, which can provide a writer with more individualized support than they might get from a larger traditional publisher.

This publishing path often requires the writer to invest a portion of their own money in the publishing process for services such as editing, cover design, typesetting, and others.

Boutique publishers are usually very friendly to their writers and are often open to negotiating royalties and letting authors maintain creative rights to their work.

Regardless of what you choose to do with your story, it is ready to go to a professional editor. You did it!

Congratulations!

Before You Go

Thank you so much for choosing the *Inkslinger – 99-Day Guided Writing Experience* to help you write your story. We sincerely hope the experience has been a good one for you. We definitely enjoyed writing it.

Our greatest joy will be to see more people who have always wanted to write a story get their stories out there for the world to read them. So, please, tell us how you did.

We want to hear from you!

If you have comments, questions, or just want to say "Hi," visit our website at www.instacks.com and go to the "Contact us" section to drop us a note. Don't forget to sign the note with "[Your Name] - Author." You earned it!

Much love,
Kimberly

www.ingramcontent.com/pod-product-compliance
Lightning Source LLC
Chambersburg PA
CBHW050725030426
42336CB00012B/1416